FIT TO CLIMB

A 16-WEEK MOUNT RAINIER
FITNESS TRAINING PROGRAM

BY JOHN COLVER

WITH

ROHIT EIPE

Fit to Climb

A 16-Week Mount Rainier Fitness Training Program

ISBN-13: 978-1978119956
ISBN-10: 197811995X

Illustrations by Maya Smith
Front Cover Photography by John Colver
Back Cover Photography by Sean Airhart and Siddharth Sriram

www.johncolver.com

Give feedback on the book at:
rohit.eipe@gmail.com and john@johncolver.com

First Edition

Printed in the U.S.A

It is not the mountain we conquer but ourselves.

—Edmund Hillary

CONTENTS

ACKNOWLEDGEMENTS

Producing a work such as *Fit to Climb* is a community effort. There are countless people who have contributed to the creation of the book, the training program, and to our own learning. Every person we have had the opportunity to climb with, train with, or to interview, has been a teacher. We are grateful for the companionship of guides and rangers on the mountain as well as for the conversations with coaches and contributors to this work.

John would like to thank his friend and *Fit to Climb* writing partner, Rohit Eipe, for his thought, effort, patience, and perseverance during the journey to complete this book.

Rohit would like to thank John Colver for re-acquainting him with running and fitness and for introducing him to mountain climbing. John has been an inspiration to him for all kinds of outdoor adventures for nearly a decade.

John and Rohit would like to thank Dr. Maya Smith for spending many hours reading, editing, providing feedback, and listening to us talk about the book. Maya also beautifully illustrated the Rainier Dozen and other exercises in the book, bringing them to life. Her contributions have been invaluable to this book.

Christine Reynolds provided some of the most thoughtful feedback we received from anyone who read a manuscript. She has had a profound impact on the final product. John and Rohit are also indebted to the folks who have read manuscripts and given feedback over the years: Shauna Balderson, Ward and Boni Buringrud, Susan Dutro, Lance Mansfield, Deborah Reber, and Jessica Webb. Their ideas, patience, and endless encouragement have made this book possible.

People who have helped significantly to support John, Rohit, and *Fit to Climb* include Karen Chaudiere, Erin Coomer, Charlie Davis,

Chris Gee, Joel Goetz, Stephanie Gundel, Tony Hoskins, Christi Krug, Daniel Letzler, Dr. Scott Marshall, Brianna Parke, Leslie Richardson, Raghu Simha, Siddharth Sriram, Lynn and John Tissell, Anna and John Ungar, and Heather and Martin de Vrieze. Over the past decade, our training, hiking, and climbing adventures with them have provided much inspiration and encouragement for this book.

Finally, John would like to acknowledge people who have provided teaching, expertise, and leadership both on and off the mountain. Our goal in offering *Fit to Climb* to readers is to provide a hands-on manual, rich with personal experience from people at the forefront of their fields in exercise physiology, professional mountain guiding, coaching, and writing. This includes leaders who have made outstanding contributions to the sport of mountaineering and who are committed to the enjoyment and success of people starting out in this life-changing activity. Thank you to Mark Anderson, Peter Anderson, Melissa Arnot, Rob Banga, Jake Beren, Sir Chris Bonington, Wolfgang Brolley, Federico "El Fede" Campanini, Zachary Cross, Jeff Dossett, George Dunn, Jason Edwards, Phil Ershler, Mike "Gator" Gauthier, Doug Goodfellow, Fernando Grajales, Casey Grom, Mike Haft, Walter Hailes, Dave Hann, Sally Hara, Joe Horiski, Randy Huntington, Tyler Jones, Karen Killian, Liesl Langley, Alisoune Lee, Paul Maier, Linden Mallory, Andres Marin, Jeff Martin, Justin Merle, Tim Niemier, Brent Okita, Michelle Van Otten, Donn Owsley, Jenni Pfafman, John and Olivia Race, Eric Remza, Paul Rosser, Minna Rudd, Woody Ryland, Dr. Robert "Brownie" Schoene, Anna Shaffer, Austin Shannon, Lakpa Rita Sherpa, Alex Van Steen, Josh Tapp, Vern Tejas, James Thornton, Tino Villanueva, Tom Vogl, Jeff Ward, Seth Waterfall, Jim Whittaker, Lou Whittaker, Peter Whittaker, and David Whyte.

John Colver and Rohit Eipe
Seattle, Washington

For my brother, Keith Anthony Colver.—JC

For Maya Smith and my parents, Mathew and Susan Eipe.—RE

SECTION 1

INTRODUCTION

CHAPTER 1

WHY CLIMB MOUNT RAINIER?

Because in the end, you won't remember the time you spent working in the office or mowing your lawn. Climb that goddamn mountain.

—Jack Kerouac

MOTIVATION FOR THE CLIMB

For many Pacific Northwest residents, climbing Mount Rainier is a lifetime ambition. The mountain is visible from Seattle, and on a clear day, sitting 14,411 feet high and 72 miles away, it dominates the skyline. Jim Whittaker, the first American to ascend Mount Everest, has called Mount Rainier, "Everyman's Everest." Given its unique challenges, it is the pinnacle of achievement for climbers from all over North America and beyond. The mountain was named for Peter Rainier, a British Naval Admiral, in 1792 by Captain George Vancouver on his exploratory voyage on the "HMS Discovery." The name, Rainier, is used extensively in

Washington, usually by organizations and businesses seeking a mark of prestige and grandeur. We have The Rainier Club, Rainier Beer, Rainier Hardware, Rainier Pizza; the list is long.

I've heard many reasons for people wanting to climb Mount Rainier. More than one person says that it looks good on a resume. Following in the footsteps of the American Lung Association, many charities have selected Mount Rainier as a goal for a fundraising event; so, people climb it as a fitness challenge and simultaneously for charity. People leave ashes, propose marriage, and even tie the knot on the summit! Phil Ershler, owner of International Mountain Guides, paraphrases Warren Miller by saying, "Climb it now, or you'll be a year older when you do!" After looking at the "giant white billboard to the south of Seattle," more than a few people have said that sooner or later they wonder what it is like up there. A business recruiter once told me, "I look for many things on a resume. An MBA is great; experience is great. And when I see Mount Rainier on a resume, it tells me that this person knows how to face fears and overcome adversity, two great traits for an employee."

According to records kept by the National Park Service, Hazard Stevens and Philemon Beecher Van Trump made the first documented successful climb of Mount Rainier on August 17, 1870. My estimate is that since that historic day, over 185,000 people have climbed the mountain. According to the National Park Service, approximately 10,000 climbers attempt the summit climb each year, and fewer than 50% succeed.

During my tenure as a Rainier guide and during coaching sessions, I notice, not infrequently, the impact that a climb can have. Climbing can touch the mind and soul. I see photographs on desks, summit certificates hanging in offices, ice axes on fireplaces or hanging on walls, carabiners from climbs used as keychains—daily reminders of the mountain. I, myself, have a rock from the summit on my desk!

So, why climb Mount Rainier? To me, it's because of the beauty, the physical challenge, the remoteness, and the chance to escape the day-to-day routine. Since I was 16 years old, I've always climbed mountains and have never tired of it. I've spent a significant portion of my life outdoors. Day or night, summer or winter, I think there is an aspect of nature for me that far transcends mountaineering. And yet, there is simply nothing like being up there in the midst of it all. Even when working on mountains I've always relished the thought of suiting-up and heading out on a glacier or into a storm. I've taken on challenging sports like running, cycling, and boxing. Running a marathon is hard, but up there on the mountain, there are no aid stations. Sometimes there are no breaks, and you keep going till the mountain lets you off it. If something goes wrong, the need for self- and team-sufficiency is absolute. You also get instant feedback. If you step wrong, you fall over, and then get up and try again, not needing to wait for a judge to tell you how you are doing. You just know, all the time.

Over the years, the people I have guided have had many reasons for embarking on this journey. For many of them, the mystery is the draw. The question, itself, evokes mystique: "Why climb Mount Rainier?" People climb for a transformational experience, to satisfy a childhood goal, in memory of someone they loved or who loved them. They climb for fitness, for health, and to experience the fierce beauty of nature. More than one person that I have asked, "Why do you do it?" has replied, "It's a search for meaning."

Many people report that the experience of being part of a team is one of the most memorable aspects of the climb. Being connected by carabiners and a thin nylon rope is certainly a bonding experience. The famous French guide and writer Gaston Rébuffat often spoke of the connectedness of everyone on the team while on the mountain.

There is danger and beauty on the mountain. With the wind blowing around you, metal points in the snow, cool moonlight reflected on ancient rock, glacial ice contrasting with the night sky above the clouds and valleys, with the jagged edge of the horizon against a backdrop of light years of stars, galaxies, and blackness beyond, it's hard for me not to feel deeply alive when I am high up on a mountain.

The allure is great. I do not guide these days, and I see the mountain from Seattle more than I feel it under my feet. Some days I ignore it; some days I soak in the view. Most days I glance southwards and feel a calm sense of contentment that I've taken the time to climb up through the clouds and explore this giant volcano that has captivated the imagination and passion of so many people. For me, there is a small sense, after each climb, of disbelief. I look back towards the peak with tired eyes and think to myself, "Goodness, did we really just do that?"

KNOWING WHAT YOU'RE GETTING INTO

After hearing about what an amazing experience it is to climb Mount Rainier, you're probably ready to start training immediately! This is good, and you'll want to reach for that passion during the hard workouts of your training program as well as on the climb itself.

Climbing Mount Rainier is a significant effort. I've heard many people say it was the hardest thing they've ever done, and I've heard others say that it was tough but not as tough as they thought it would be. How you train will make a difference not only to your summit success, but also in terms of where you land on that spectrum. My wish is that you don't just gain the conditioning to be able to go to the summit and back, but that you also enjoy the experience. I've had days on the mountain where it was hard work, and there have been others when at the peak of my fitness, I would stroll across the ice of the crater, walk up the red-brown pumice trail while listening to the steam vents, and just marvel at the beauty of it all: the sun reflecting off the Pacific Ocean in the distance, Seattle to the north, both Canada and Oregon visible on a clear day.

Today, some would say that, in relation to the weather, you can stack the odds of success in your favor. What has not changed, and I imagine never will, is that the only way for most people to reach the summit of Mount Rainier is by shouldering a heavy pack and physically putting one foot in front of the other. Mount Rainier National Park's regulations forbid the use of porters, livestock, or motorized vehicles on trails. There are no lifts, cable cars, or roads to any of the base camps on Mount Rainier.

Consequently, for a climber to reach the summit of Mount Rainier involves a push of 9,000 feet over 9 miles, carrying a sizeable backpack weighing anywhere from 35 to 60 pounds. By any standard in international climbing, this is a tremendous effort in a short space of time. For most people, the actual climb will consist of a 6-hour trek, followed by a rest at Camp Muir, before heading out on a summit climb that will take between 12 and 16 hours to complete.

A typical 4- or 5-day trip looks like the following:

- Day 1: Orientation at Mount Rainier National Park
- Day 2: A full day of mountaineering training
- Day 3: Trek from Paradise (5,400 feet) to Camp Muir (10,060 feet)
- Day 4: Adjust to altitude at Camp Muir and 2-hour hike (the 4-day trip skips over this day)
- Day 5: Summit climb (14,411 feet) and return to Paradise

Mount Rainier is frequently described as the toughest endurance climb in the lower 48 states of the United States. It is a uniquely challenging mountain to climb, specifically because of its geographical location in relation to the Pacific Ocean, its northerly latitude, and its inclusion in the maritime temperate climate of the Pacific Northwest.

Practically, the upper slopes of Mount Rainier are an Arctic island in a temperate region. On a typical summer's day, tourists at the Paradise Visitor Center (5,400 feet) will be sweltering in 80-degree heat. 9,000 feet above them, the temperature will be well below freezing and likely accompanied by storm-force winds. It is a mountain of extreme conditions.

Another unique aspect of Mount Rainier is the preponderance of large glaciers that exist here due to the high levels of rain and snow driven from the Pacific Ocean. This makes Mount Rainier a sought-after training ground for Himalayan climbers from around the world. In the winter, Arctic fronts blast Mount Rainier with fierce winter storms. In the early summer, the winds shift to the southwest, bringing the "Pineapple Express" and other tropical systems from the South Pacific.

Mountains of a similar grandeur throughout the world generally sit on continental plains far from major oceans. This is true in North America (the Rockies), Europe (Mont Blanc, Mount Elbrus), and Asia (the Baltoro Muztagh, which is home to K2, and the Himalayan ranges). Only on the eastern coast of Asia and the west coast of North America are such high peaks found so close to oceans. In fact, Mount Rainier is fewer than 60 miles, as the crow flies, from the Pacific Ocean. This proximity to a vast ocean adds another serious component to climbing the mountain: weather. Conditions at any time of the year are unpredictable at best and capricious at worst. Many will battle weather on this peak, and some will not survive.

Challenging whiteout conditions with snowstorms occur all year around, even during the regular climbing season between May and September. Unfortunately, weather and snow conditions cannot be controlled. I can promise you that the guides do not worry about them, and you shouldn't either. Trust that you will be climbing with a world-class guide team, and they will make the right decision based on all the information available to them. Weather forecasting and avalanche prediction systems have improved over the years, and this has helped lessen risk. Electronic navigational tools such as Global Positioning System (GPS) have made route-finding more successful for many climbers.

Mount Rainier's location within 2 hours of a major metropolitan area, Seattle, is another reason it is such a popular training ground for climbers around the world. Its extremes in weather, abundance of glaciers, and an endurance climb of over 9,000 feet, combined with the growing interest in mountain climbing over the past several decades, have made Mount Rainier the jewel of alpine glacier climbing and the most visited in the lower 48 states. Weather, conditions, skills, and experience play a role in the difficulty of the climb, but as the National Park Service reminds climbers, fitness plays the biggest part in determining summit success.

WHAT THE TRAINING LOOKS LIKE

A few years ago, I was supporting a team of climbers training for an expedition to Mount Kilimanjaro, and their climb was coming up soon. We'd been cold, wet, and fatigued. There had been aching muscles, a few blisters, trial and error with gear, sore shoulders from backpacks, and the occasional bump and bruise. We were out in all kinds of weather and "burning the headlamps at both ends of the day." There was some apprehension, too. "Will I make it?" "Is it worth the money and effort?" "Will the mountain hurt me?" These questions are natural.

I think it is worth the time, money, and effort. It would be hard to hide my bias, but I believe that there is a reward to mountain climbing that does not come with many other noble and exciting sports. I've personally felt the exhilaration of crossing the finish line in marathons, pushing through the heat and hills of Ironman triathlons, and knowing the uplifting power of team sports. Yet for all of the wonderful memories and experiences, nothing has an impact on me like mountaineering. It grabs me from start to finish; it commands attention with its risks and consequences. If a person is looking for an easy pursuit, this may not be it—neither the training nor the summit climb. It takes commitment, and the level of commitment deepens the experience.

The *Fit to Climb* training program is a step-by-step, 16-week training experience, with moderate, consistent, and gradual gains. The training is like a successful climb: it requires measured effort, being in control, and always paying attention to balance and self-care. On the other hand, it will be arduous, and especially towards the end, will require a solid investment of time.

This is a good point at which to introduce a central concept for the training program in this book. Moderation and consistency are critical factors in athletic success. Modern culture has not done a great job of educating people on health and fitness. Much of what takes place every day in gyms and some fitness programs is based on outdated catch phrases like "no pain no gain," or on ill-conceived ideas that pit one type of training against another. Climbing a mountain demands true functional fitness and will test every aspect of that fitness. But the nature of the climb itself is measured and the pace is consistent. The same is true for the entire *Fit to Climb* program. The goal is not to simply work hard—though you certainly will do that. The goal is to become very good at the skills in the particular areas of fitness that will carry your body 14,000 feet above sea level into a very challenging environment. As you progress through the training program, you will establish a focused and careful consistency, which is exactly the mindset that will create success on summit day.

For most of the weeks of training, you'll do 1 dedicated strength session, a couple of cardiovascular training sessions, a cross-training workout, and a hike. You will learn the Rainier Dozen, a set of calisthenic exercises that you may well do for the rest of your life. You will learn a circuit workout and perform fitness tests to measure your progress. During the 16 weeks, you'll learn a lot about mountaineering, conditioning, and yourself. It won't consume your life, but the training schedule will provide a structure and rhythm to your life outside of work and family. You will not need to set foot in a gym, but it will feel like an adventure from day 1. You'll start in one season and end in another. The adventure of training for and climbing Mount Rainier will be an indelible experience that can never be taken away.

CHAPTER 2

HOW TO USE THIS BOOK

Welcome to your mountain training adventure! As you embark on the next 16 weeks, there are a few things that you should know so that you can get the most out of this book.

WHO THIS BOOK IS FOR

This book is for readers that have made the decision to climb Mount Rainier and are looking for the best way to prepare themselves to get there. Climbing Mount Rainier is a significant achievement, and this training program is hard work. If you put in the effort outlined in this book, you will give yourself the best possible chance to successfully summit the mountain. You will learn new exercises and incorporate them into a training regimen that will steadily train your body (and mind) to climb Mount Rainier. Preparing for a successful climb is a journey that begins well before you set foot on the mountain.

This book does not teach the technical aspects of mountain climbing, such as how to perform an ice axe arrest, how to travel with a team on a rope, or how to use a crampon. I believe that this is best taught via in-person training. Therefore, this book is intended to be used by a climber who is planning their expedition with a guide service or an experienced mountain guide. In the Seattle area, many guide services offer summit climbs that include a full day of mountaineering training, which will incorporate all the above topics and more.

I firmly believe that most readers can put in 16 weeks of diligent effort and put themselves in a good position to have a successful climb. The first 9 weeks of the program build up your fitness base quite gradually. If you are diligent with the workouts and practice self-care as you progress, these first two phases should not be too taxing for most. However, if you are struggling to perform some of the workouts in this book or simply anticipate that you will need extra conditioning to be successful in the first few weeks, you should give yourself that additional time. This may involve starting the program a few weeks earlier and repeating any week that feels unduly hard.

Even the best-laid plans sometimes come undone. If you miss a workout or two because of a minor cold, this will not affect your overall training. I would recommend that you simply skip those workouts and continue with the training program on the day that you feel better. However, if you have a major illness that takes two weeks out of your training or you are unable to perform the hard workouts, then you may have to make the difficult decision not to climb in the year that you are training. Make an honest evaluation of your fitness level and the time remaining, and proceed from there.

Lastly, note that the peak climbing season for Mount Rainier runs from May through September, though there are certainly climbs that occur outside of that time period. Depending on when your climb is, you should work backwards about 4 months to give yourself time to read through the book before starting your training. Add in a few extra weeks if you anticipate missing some critical workouts due to work or travel plans. An ideal reading of the book takes place sometime between

December and March to establish a plan for your training adventure. You should return to the "Training Program" section during your training to refresh your memory for each week ahead, and refer to any other supporting information as you need to.

LAYOUT OF THE BOOK

So far, in Section 1: "Introduction," you have read about the allure of climbing Mount Rainier, what you are getting into, and about the high-level structure of the training program. The rest of this chapter talks about how the book is organized and has some tips on how to read it for your particular situation.

Section 2: "Preparation for Training" gives you some background on the kinds of athletic competencies for a successful Mount Rainier climb, as well as provides instruction on some of the exercises you will encounter in the weeks ahead. "What Type of Training Is Important" gives you an understanding of the three types of fitness you will develop during your mountain training—aerobic, anaerobic, and strength training—and how they all fit together. The "Rainier Dozen" chapter consists of 12 exercises that you will perform daily over the next 16 weeks and that are designed to serve both as a warm-up and to continuously build your fitness. For each exercise, I have included a verbal description and pictures to show you how to perform them. It is also a good idea to look at videos of these exercises online to help with good form.

Section 3: "Support for Successful Training" is all about the ways you will want to support and nourish your body and mind in order to manage the rigors of your training and get the most out of the 16 weeks. "Nutrition: Fuel for the Journey" talks about the kinds of foods you will need during training and on the climb, as well as a cheat-sheet of what I carry with me when I climb. The chapter on "Equipment" talks about the basic gear you will need: the "10 essentials," backpacks, footwear, clothing, and safety equipment. As mentioned earlier in this chapter, I will not talk about technical climbing gear; you should seek out in-person mountaineering training for this. Lastly, but perhaps most importantly, "Self-Care and Recovery" discusses some techniques for managing the stress that the training program will place on your body and your mind. There are some examples of good stretches in here, as well a number of other ideas to stay injury free during the training. Additionally, there are some ideas that you can try out on your longer hikes that will help you on your mountain climb.

Section 4: "The Training Program" is the core of the book. It is organized into 4 phases: the Adaptation, Foundation, Peak, and Expedition phases. The section begins with an overview of the entire training program. Next, I provide some information for you to plan each kind of workout. I recommend that you do this early on so that you can focus on your training when you get into it! You will also find a table that describes the entire training program at a quick glance, in case you want to take it all in at once. Finally, I walk you through each phase and week of the training program, with detailed descriptions of each workout. At the beginning of each phase is a pulse check—a time to take stock of how your training is progressing and make any adjustments necessary.

Section 5: "The Climb" is all about your mountain expedition. "Summit Day" is a description of a typical 5-day climb of Mount Rainier on the popular Disappointment Cleaver route. Depending on the conditions at the time that you climb and the specific guide service with which you work, your experience may be slightly different, but my hope is to inspire you nonetheless.

After some closing words in the "Epilogue," you will find a collection of nuggets of wisdom that I have gathered over my years of climbing in the appendix, "37 Things They Never Tell You before You Climb." You can't prepare for everything on the mountain, but hopefully you can be prepared for most things that the mountain will throw your way.

SECTION 2

PREPARATION FOR TRAINING

CHAPTER 3

WHAT TYPE OF TRAINING
IS IMPORTANT

In this chapter, I will introduce you to the three athletic pillars of your training program. As you read this information, note that some of it might seem overwhelming at this stage. Rest assured that you will be guided in future chapters as to how to achieve these competencies with instructions for specific workouts.

As you set out to train for Mount Rainier, you will develop multiple fitness competencies. Many of these will improve in concert with each other. For instance, as you increase leg strength, you will improve balance. As you improve coordination, you will increase overall energy efficiency.

Each person possesses varying amounts of these different attributes. The good news is that some of these attributes are more valuable than others. This applies in any sport. For Mount Rainier climbers, the most valuable attributes are aerobic endurance, anaerobic endurance, and strength. Let's consider each of these in turn.

AEROBIC ENDURANCE

WHY YOU NEED IT

Here is the definition of the term "aerobic," from the Merriam-Webster Dictionary.

1. living, active, or occurring only in the presence of oxygen <aerobic respiration>
2. involving, utilizing, or increasing oxygen consumption for metabolic processes in the body

Aerobic endurance stands above all else as the predominant aspect of fitness required for a successful expedition. During aerobic exercise, your muscles burn carbohydrates and fats in the presence of oxygen, and this can be sustained by the body for a long period of time. You have to develop the aerobic capacity to have the ability and energy for the long, steady effort that will be required. There are no shortcuts to this process. However, the good news is that the way to build aerobic endurance is to train at an intensity level that is comfortable and enjoyable.

In other words, let's go for a walk!

HOW TO DEVELOP AEROBIC ENDURANCE: THE LONG HIKE

The way to develop aerobic endurance is by performing activities that require a moderate effort over a long period of time. In each week's training, you'll find a long-distance hike. The length of this hike will increase over the course of the training program, until towards the end, you will be testing your aerobic endurance over nearly 9 hours. This is the core activity of this training program, akin to the long run in marathon training.

If you find yourself unable to hike every week or weekend, then a long bike ride, cross-country ski session, or run will provide benefits that are close to that of hiking. In a pinch, they can be substituted for a couple of the hikes. While they are close in effectiveness, they will not provide the same overall benefit to your mountain readiness. For instance, developing balance and coordination out on the trail is best achieved by actually getting out on the trail. So, I encourage you to make the long hike an integral part of your training program and to look at the other activities above as cross-training opportunities.

It is important, however, not to substitute cardiovascular endurance training with the other kinds mentioned in this chapter: anaerobic or strength training. Remember that the main requirement for climbing Mount Rainier is to travel by foot over 18 miles with over 9,000 feet gained in elevation, all while carrying a backpack. There is simply no substitute for aerobic cardiovascular training.

I'd like to make a clarification on the location of these hikes. Hiking at a nearby mountain, national park, or wilderness trail is a great way to get acquainted with some of the terrain and conditions you will encounter on Mount Rainier. However, the primary goal of this part of the training is to build aerobic endurance through long stretches of moderate activity. If you are situated in a city or town that has easy access to alpine hikes, make good use of that opportunity. But if you don't have easy access to hills or mountains, get creative with urban hikes in the hillier parts of your city.

WHAT IT TAKES

Aerobic endurance training takes time. First, you need to allow the time to perform the practice sessions. In week 1, this is only 1 hour for the long hike. However, the Mount Rainier summit climb will require up to 14 hours in almost a single push, and your training will extend to 9 hours of hiking at its peak. The other part of the time consideration is that in order to have a reasonable progression of effort, you need to start many months before the expedition. This is the primary reason for the selection of 16 weeks as the length of the standard *Fit to Climb* program. It's true that some people train in less time and some people will require more time to gradually build up fitness. However, in my experience of hands-on coaching with climbers, if a person of average fitness spends 16 weeks on training, they will be successful in attaining the endurance required for the summit climb.

As the program goes on, your aerobic endurance hikes will become progressively longer. If you have ever trained for a running marathon or cycling event, you will be familiar with this type of progression. Some readers may be thinking, "Why not start with longer hikes?" One of the benefits of a slow progression is to allow your ligaments, tendons, and muscles to adapt to the increasing stress caused by being on the trail for long periods. The gradual progression trains all of these systems simultaneously. Be careful to not be over-ambitious too early. Overloading the body's system too soon in a training program can lead to injury and illness. As a coaching mentor of mine likes to remind his students, "You can take a cake that is designed to be baked for 50 minutes at 300 degrees and bake it for 30 minutes at 500 degrees. But you might not like the results!" It's better to (slightly) under-train than to over-train.

ANAEROBIC ENDURANCE

Why You Need It

Here is the definition of the word "anaerobic," from the Merriam-Webster dictionary.

1. living, active, occurring, or existing in the absence of free oxygen <anaerobic respiration>
2. of, relating to, or being activity in which the body incurs an oxygen debt <anaerobic exercise>

The goal of a mountain leader is to maintain a steady pace, effectively putting every team member on cruise control. However, the reality of climbing is that sometimes everybody will need to move quickly. This could be because of hazardous terrain, inclement weather, or a ticking clock. Speed is not the only reason for developing anaerobic endurance. Steep, uneven terrain—both on ice and rock—as well as the thin air add a component of difficulty, which, for even the best mountain climber causes the heart rate to increase past your comfort zone. The first purpose of anaerobic endurance training, therefore, is to prepare the body and mind for the times during the climb when you may need to make a short, hard effort.

The second purpose of anaerobic endurance training is to raise the anaerobic threshold so that you effectively extend the range of your aerobic capacity. Briefly, a person's anaerobic threshold (or lactate threshold) is the point of exercise intensity at which their muscles begin to produce lactic acid faster than it can be broken down. Exercise cannot be sustained for very long above the anaerobic threshold. For example, if your anaerobic threshold today is 150 beats per minute (BPM) and your heart is beating at 160 BPM while on a climb, you're going to reach exhaustion in a matter of minutes. However, if your anaerobic threshold is 170 BPM and your heart is running at 160 BPM, you will be able to sustain this effort for a much longer time—theoretically an infinite amount of time—assuming you can stay fueled and hydrated. To further highlight the importance of this fact, know that having a sufficient level of anaerobic endurance training very often means that a climber will be able to ease through a difficult section of the climb and continue to the summit, rather than reaching a point of absolute fatigue and needing to stop and return to camp.

How to Develop Anaerobic Endurance: Interval Training

Your anaerobic threshold increases as you perform high-intensity training. Specifically, in order to accomplish the goal of increasing your anaerobic threshold in this training program, you will use high-intensity interval training.

High-intensity interval training is a training technique employed in many sports. It refers to a training session where periods of relatively high-intensity effort, followed by rest or lower-intensity effort, are repeated. You can do this kind of interval training on stairs, hills, a gym machine, or a bicycle. The sessions are short, intense, and highly effective. During the Foundation and Peak phases of this program, these sessions will play an important role in conditioning you for the climb.

Basic interval training involves short, measured intervals of effort and rest. Multiple versions of interval training on stairs are included in this training program. I also include a version that can be done on trails, for a bit of variety, starting in week 12. Look for all of these in the weeks and chapters ahead.

WHAT IT TAKES

Depending on the phase of training, 1 to 2 sessions per week is optimal. Choose days of the week where you're likely to be fully rested and recovered. Avoid doing back-to-back sessions as you'll need a day or two to recover after the intense effort.

STRENGTH

WHY YOU NEED IT

The question of how to define strength is a complex one. In the context of *Fit to Climb*, strength training refers to activities and practices geared towards developing muscle strength required for both general and specific demands of climbing the mountain. General conditioning needs, such as core strength, will help you make more efficient use of your time on the mountain. They will also help to reduce the risk of fatigue and injuries. More specific strength needs, such as strong legs and a strong back, are required in order to cope with the specific rigors of mountaineering such as carrying your pack for extended periods of time while ascending or descending on uneven terrain. In short, the various aspects of strength should work together. In turn, the strength you develop needs to be backed up by aerobic and anaerobic endurance to be able to efficiently and rapidly supply oxygen to your muscles.

Three important areas of strength training are maximal strength, strength endurance (stamina), and explosive strength (agility). A way to consider the difference of these types of strength is to imagine standing in front of a large log. A measure of maximal strength would be the ability to pick up the log. If you were to repeatedly step on and off the log, you would be limited by your muscle endurance (stamina). To jump over the log would be a test of your agility.

The order of priority in strength training for mountaineering is muscle endurance, followed by maximal strength, followed by explosive strength. You need high levels of muscle endurance in your legs to be able to continually make one step after the other. You need maximal strength to efficiently carry your pack as well as to tackle more technical or steep sections. Explosive strength is rarely a factor in success; however, if you need to accomplish an ice axe arrest or to jump over a crevasse, you will certainly be reliant on your agility.

In theory, you can train one type of strength at a time; however, in practice you are always using all three in a given workout. As you develop competency in one area there are natural gains in the other two. This is especially true of the holistic approach to strength training taken in *Fit to Climb*.

HOW TO DEVELOP STRENGTH: THE RAINIER DOZEN AND CIRCUIT TRAINING

There are many effective ways to train strength. The quote, "There are many paths to the top of the mountain, but the view is always the same," comes to mind. Wide-ranging examples such as hiking and climbing, weight training, yoga, or kick-boxing all contribute to increasing strength. Popular methods such as Cross-Fit and the Barre Method can be good contributors to mountaineering strength. Military teams and firefighters use calisthenics and circuit training to achieve functional strength.

The *Fit to Climb* method is designed to be simple, efficient in terms of time, and absent of the need for unnecessary equipment or expense. The different components of strength training have to fit well with the rest of the program in terms of intensity and timing. Most importantly, though, the training has to work. With all of the training, I urge you to approach this work with the mindset of a professional. Adopt an attitude that starts by saying, "I am going to the top of the mountain." This will naturally lead you to the question of, "What do I need to do in order to accomplish this?" This is the approach taken in deciding the *Fit to Climb* strength training method.

Fit to Climb approaches the matter of strength training in two ways. First, it does so through a daily workout called the Rainier Dozen, and second, through dedicated strength training sessions once a week. The Rainier Dozen is a workout that you can (and ideally will) do every day for the next 4 months, and it will gradually build a base of core strength, stamina, and agility. The focused strength training sessions will take this to the next level, helping you raise your level of maximal strength. Both of these are designed to build the strength necessary for you to reach the summit. As with all effective training, there may be days where it feels a bit basic compared with the latest fitness trend. It is important, however, to stay focused on getting strong in ways that will help you at 13,000 feet when your body is tired and the wind is threatening to blow you off the mountain!

WHAT IT TAKES

The Rainier Dozen is a set of exercises that you will perform every day for the next 4 months, and the next chapter is devoted entirely to this topic. The strength-focused training sessions comprise some fundamental strength training exercises that you perform in circuits: 40 seconds on and 20 seconds off. You'll start with 2 sets of the exercises, gradually building up to 4 sets. By that time, you'll have the strength you need to make a successful summit.

PUTTING IT ALL TOGETHER

The question of how to pull together a training plan from the myriad of ideas and methods available can be exciting. It can also be overwhelming. The *Fit to Climb* method is rooted in two key principles: "Keep it simple" and "Do what works." Long hikes build aerobic endurance. Stair training increases your anaerobic threshold and builds a bit of strength. The Rainier Dozen exercises and focused strength circuit training build the various components of strength you need. Put together in a 16-week program, these different workouts will be successful if followed.

This program is not designed with perfection in mind, nor is it the most complicated program available. It is practically designed for the rigors of climbing Mount Rainier. As such, it accepts the most basic of mountaineering tenets: the mountain is unpredictable. As the weeks ahead go by, you will not only become physically fit, you will—as a result of the variety in your training—become very adaptable to the ambiguous, fickle demands that mountaineering places on every climber. Think of it as "mountain-proofing" yourself. As you progress, enjoy the process of taking every aspect of your fitness to new levels.

A fundamental concept that will drive the entire 16-week training program is that you will increase the intensity or length of the workouts each week, but you won't dramatically increase both elements in one week. This honors a time-tested training theory of changing one thing at a time, so that you can feel the incremental gains of the additional training while avoiding the danger of overtraining.

In fact, during most weeks, you will increase the length of workouts by 1 repetition, 1 set of stairs, or a few additional minutes. In some weeks, the intensity will jump up as you introduce a new challenging workout, such as the fitness test in week 4 or high-intensity stair interval training in week 6. As you approach these points in the program that represent increases in intensity, pay particular attention to self-care and how your body is responding to the new workouts. For a detailed discussion of overtraining, see the "Self-Care and Recovery" chapter in Section 3.

MAKING THIS PROGRAM WORK FOR YOU

People from all over the world and all walks of life climb Mount Rainier. While the basic cornerstones described above need to be in place for most people's success, no two training programs are alike. Personally, I find that part of the adventure is planning the training around the very real factors and restrictions that normal day-to-day life imposes. The training program for an inter-continental airline pilot whom I trained naturally looked very different from a high-tech executive or a stay-at-home parent, and the summit register of Mount Rainier is full of people who fit into these and other lifestyle categories. The trick is balance, which is easier said than done. A careful look at the priorities in your lives—family, work, and other commitments—combined with the training requirements for this adventure, will be both revealing and empowering. What matters is that you focus on the training priorities that are going to make the biggest difference on the climb.

You may go into the climb lacking a little strength or having not done as much endurance training as you expected you could. In my experience, rarely does a person complete 100% of the training. But if the plan is solid and the direction is good, you will see significant gains in the areas that will help you reach your goal.

Take the time to sit down with the training plan (or at least the overview), and see how it lays out in your life over the next 4 months. Each week, plan out the week ahead: when you'll have time for the interval and strength training sessions, where and with whom you'll complete your long hikes. A good practice is to complete the workouts at the same time every day, if possible. Make the Rainier Dozen part of your daily routine. Before you know it, you'll be putting on your boots for your climb up Mount Rainier!

CHAPTER 4

RAINIER DOZEN

This chapter provides instruction on how to complete the Rainier Dozen exercises. The Rainier Dozen is a key building block of the *Fit to Climb* training program. As you will be performing these exercises many times over the next few months, it is worth taking the time to understand and practice the exercises a few times in the early weeks or perhaps even before the official start of your training program. Return to this chapter as many times as you need until the movements are natural.

The Rainier Dozen is based upon the Daily Dozen, as featured in *Fit By Nature: The Adventx Twelve-Week Outdoor Fitness Program.* The original Daily Dozen was in fact a 12-exercise routine performed by the 82nd Airborne troops during training in preparation for the Second World War. The concept is a simple, fun, and highly effective way of adding strength training to a fitness program.

An often-heard comment from my clients is how surprising it is that 12 minutes of exercise make a difference. The fact is that 12 minutes per day add up to almost 1.5 hours per week, or 6 hours a month. Viewed in this way, you can start to see the value of this routine, which will become an integral part of your training program. It is my recommendation that for the next 16 weeks, you perform the Rainier Dozen every day. Because the workout is short, it will not tax your body even on rest days. After just a couple of weeks of performing this short exercise routine, you will notice significant benefits to your overall strength and movement skills.

When you do it is up to you; however, it is designed to be done the first thing in the morning. One of the benefits of this approach is that you will carry this all-body workout into the rest of your day. Every subsequent movement, whether it be getting in and out of the car, walking up stairs, or reaching down to pick something up will solidify the quality movement patterns that you have practiced earlier that day. As a practical tip, I know of many people who do the Rainier Dozen (or the Daily Dozen) in the kitchen while brewing a pot of coffee or tea. Done this way, the workout has virtually no impact on your daily schedule but has a tremendous impact on your fitness.

RAINIER DOZEN INSTRUCTIONS

The Rainier Dozen exercises are:

1. Steam engines
2. Three-quarter squats
3. Lunges
4. Arm extenders
5. Triceps dips
6. Deep squats
7. Steam engines lying down
8. Mountain climbers

9. Push-ups

10. Russian twists

11. Ranger crawls

12. 8-point body builders

For each of the exercises, your goal is to perform 10 of them and then take a few seconds of rest before transitioning to the next exercise. For some of the more advanced exercises—such as 8-point body builders— it would be a good idea to start with a lower number and work your way up to 10 over a few weeks.

Additionally, keep in mind that when starting out, it is prudent to focus on quality rather than quantity. Review the pictures and descriptions for each exercise carefully. Try to perform the exercises with the best form you can, and work your way up to a greater number of repetitions as the weeks progress. Focusing on the right form also gives you a baseline to gauge your fitness improvements as time progresses. If you are able to comfortably do 5 push-ups with the right form in week 1, and can do 10 push-ups without lowering your body all the way in week 4, this may or may not indicate an increase in fitness level. However, if you can do 5 push-ups with the right form in week 1, and can do 10 push-ups with the right form in week 4, you know that you have made significant strides and are on a good path. There are also many excellent video resources on the Internet about the right form with which to perform these exercises.

1. Steam Engines

As a compound exercise, steam engines stretch the hamstrings, abdominal muscles, and back muscles in several directions. They help you develop a sense of balance, which will help you on the varying terrain of the mountain.

Stand with your feet shoulder-width apart and your hands clasped behind your head. Lift your left knee while simultaneously twisting your body to bring your right elbow towards your left knee. Maintain a smooth motion while keeping the muscles of your core engaged. Return to the starting position and then switch the movement to the other side, using your right knee and left elbow. Repeat 10 times.

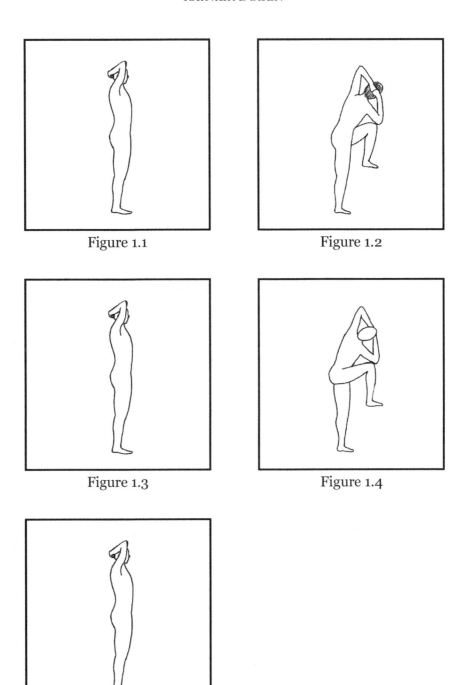

Figure 1.1

Figure 1.2

Figure 1.3

Figure 1.4

Figure 1.5

2. THREE-QUARTER SQUATS

Squats definitely build muscles in your legs (particularly your hamstrings, quadriceps, glutes, and calves), but what might not be as obvious is that they are a great full-body exercise. They're also functionally similar to actions you will need to take repeatedly on the mountain, such as getting up or sitting down at camp or during breaks on your climb.

Start by standing upright, with your feet about shoulder-width apart. You can keep your hands on your hips, or for a slightly greater challenge, you can extend them out in front of or above you. Bend your knees, push your hips back, and lower yourself as if you were about to sit down in a chair. It's important to keep your knees in line with or behind your toes, which is why I use the chair analogy. Hold the position for 2 seconds, and then push with your heels to return to the upright position. Repeat 10 times.

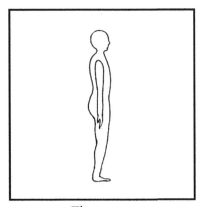

Figure 2.1

Figure 2.2

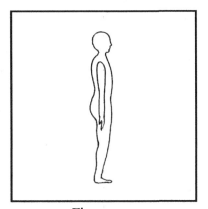

Figure 2.3

3. LUNGES

The lunge is a good lower-body exercise that trains a few different muscle groups, primarily including the glutes, hamstrings, and quadriceps. It also engages the calves for stabilization. These large muscles will all play a significant part in a successful mountain expedition.

While performing the lunge, keep your upper body as straight as possible with your shoulders relaxed. Engage your core. From a standing position, step forward using your left foot. Lower your hips until both knees are bent at just less than a 90-degree angle. Your left (front) knee should not extend past your ankle. Hold this position for a second or longer if you like and then return to the starting position. As you do so, focus on maintaining your balance. Repeat with the other side. Both sides together count as 1. Repeat for 10.

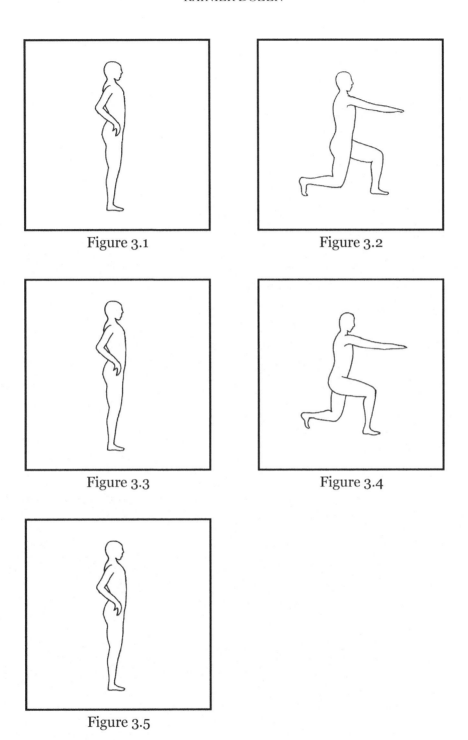

Figure 3.1

Figure 3.2

Figure 3.3

Figure 3.4

Figure 3.5

4. ARM EXTENDERS

The arm extender develops strength primarily in your shoulder muscles as well as the chest and upper-back muscles. The benefits of this are that it will lessen fatigue while carrying a backpack and increase endurance when using an ice axe and hiking poles.

Standing upright, start with the arms and elbows raised to shoulder level and with your arms bent at the elbows. Your palms should be horizontal and overlapping each other right in front of your face. Rotate your shoulders outwards and move your hands away from each other in a short motion, and bring them back in. Repeat three times, and on the fourth time, completely extend the arms straight out to each side. Pause for a second, and repeat the entire exercise 10 times.

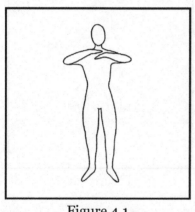

Figure 4.1

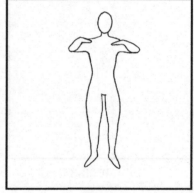

Figure 4.2

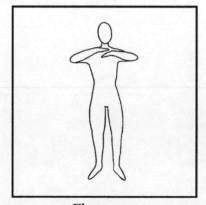

Figure 4.3

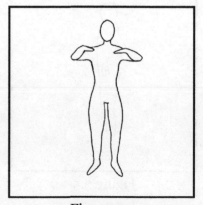

Figure 4.4

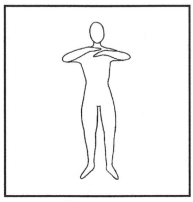

Figure 4.5

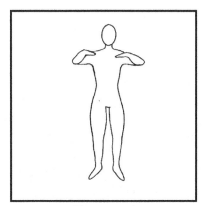

Figure 4.6

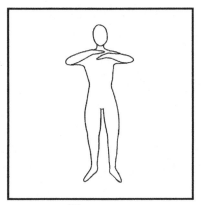

Figure 4.7

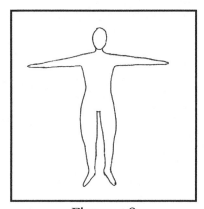

Figure 4.8

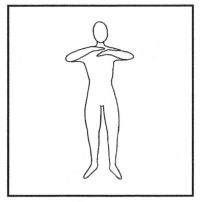

Figure 4.9

5. TRICEPS DIPS

The triceps dip develops, well, your triceps. Having strong triceps will come in handy when you have to use ice tools or when making a repetitive motion thousands of times while using your hiking poles.

Find a solid object, such as a short wall, some stairs, or a bench. Facing away from it, place your hands behind your body on the edge of the object. Your legs can be straight, or to reduce the resistance, they can be bent at the knees. With your core muscles engaged, lower your body until the angle between your forearm and upper arm is approximately 100 degrees. Be careful not to lower yourself further than this, because doing so will place undue strain on your shoulders. Reverse the movement to raise yourself to the start position. Repeat 10 times.

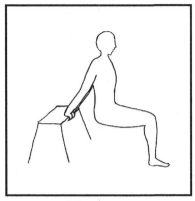

Figure 5.1

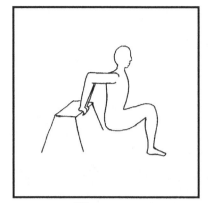

Figure 5.2

Figure 5.3

6. DEEP SQUATS

Deep squats (also known as sumo squats or plié squats) work many of the same muscles as regular squats, and in addition, help to stabilize the hips and strengthen the inner thighs. Therefore, in addition to all of the benefits of regular squats, you are also developing stability and balance.

Start in an upright position, and place your feet wider than shoulder-width apart. Your knees and toes should be pointed outward at a 45-degree angle. You can also hold your arms above your head for a little extra difficulty. Push your hips back, and squat down until your knees are at a 90-degree angle or your thighs are parallel to the ground. Keep your chest up during this motion to maintain good form. Hold the position for 2 seconds, and then push through your heels to rise back to the upright position. Repeat 10 times.

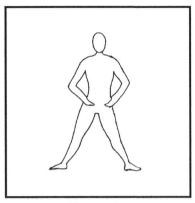

Figure 6.1

Figure 6.2

Figure 6.3

7. STEAM ENGINES LYING DOWN

This variant of the steam engine has many of the same benefits of the standing steam engine: primarily working your abdominal muscles, your external obliques, your hamstrings, and your lower back.

Lie on your back, and extend your legs out, holding your feet a few inches above the ground. Place your hands behind your head. Bring your left knee in towards your chest, while simultaneously bringing your right elbow towards the left knee. Try to touch your elbow to the opposite knee as you do so, but take care not to strain your head forward as you do so; it would be better to go as far as you comfortably can. Repeat on the other side. Once each on both sides counts as 1. Repeat this for 10 times.

To increase the intensity of this exercise after a few weeks, you can try the following "3-and-hold" variation. Starting on the left, touch your left knee to your right elbow, then your right knee to your left elbow, then left knee to right elbow again, and hold in this pose (with your right leg extended) for about 2 seconds. This counts as 1 repetition. Repeat for 10 times, alternating between starting each repetition with the left knee or right knee (you would be holding the opposite leg extended during the pause with each alternation).

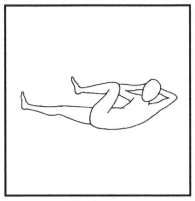

Figure 7.1

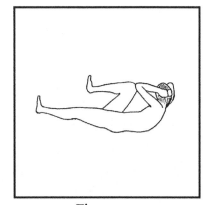

Figure 7.2

Figure 7.3

8. MOUNTAIN CLIMBERS

How could the mountain climber exercise not be good for mountain climbing! The mountain climber is a great exercise for core strength, hip flexor extension, agility in the calves, and strength in the feet and ankles. For the mountain athlete, this translates to improved flexibility, coordination, strength, and endurance—all of which are required during the stepping-up motion.

Start out in the plank position; that is, balance your upper body on your palms with your shoulders directly above, and try to maintain a straight line between your shoulders and your heels. Bring your right foot forward as if you were in the starting blocks of a 100-meter sprint. From here, simply alternate with your left and right legs as if running or bounding—or clambering up a mountain—in place. The length of the movement can be short or long depending on your level of ability. One "step" each with both feet counts as 1. Repeat 10 times.

Figure 8.1

Figure 8.2

Figure 8.3

Figure 8.4

9. PUSH-UPS

Push-ups are an excellent exercise to build strength all over your body. They do so by activating multiple muscle groups such as your biceps, triceps, lower back, core, and others. These are all muscles you engage while hiking. Push-ups raise your overall level of strength and also engage stabilizing muscles to support your body while doing the exercise. There are many variations of the push-up that you can use to ease into them slowly or to increase the difficulty.

Start in a plank position with your hands and toes slightly wider than shoulder-width apart. Try to keep your body as straight as possible between shoulders and heels. Your arms should be pointing straight down. Lower yourself in a steady motion until your elbows are at about a 90-degree angle or your chest just grazes the ground. Pause slightly, and then raise yourself back to the starting position. An ideal breathing rhythm is to inhale while lowering your body and exhale while pushing back up.

You can increase the width between your feet or spread your fingers apart to slightly decrease the difficulty. You can also rest on your knees (and imagine a straight line between your shoulders and your knees) to start out more easily, or perform a push-up with your hands on a park bench or couch instead. At the other end of the spectrum—to increase difficulty—you can try reversing the elevation (toes on a low bench and hands on the ground) or bringing your hands closer together to make a diamond between thumbs and index fingers.

Figure 9.1

Figure 9.2

Figure 9.3

10. Russian Twists

Russian twists train the core muscles in a torsional plane. This is beneficial because it mimics a number of movements that take place on the climb, such as putting on and taking off a pack or reaching for gear while taking a break. In addition, improved core strength will help you throughout the climb.

Start in a sitting position, lean back slightly with your legs crossed at the ankles. Placing both hands together, reach to the left and touch both hands to the ground; then reach to the right and touch both hands to the ground. Repeat 10 times. This exercise can be done with the feet touching the ground or elevated; the elevated version will be more challenging.

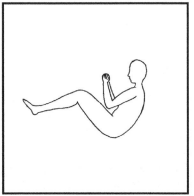

Figure 10.1

Figure 10.2

Figure 10.3

Figure 10.4

11. RANGER CRAWLS

Ranger crawls train the lower core muscles, including abdominals, lower back, hip flexors, and stabilizer muscles. If you ever have to do an ice axe arrest (lying on the ground and using an ice axe to prevent sliding), you'll be using all of the muscles that the ranger crawl trains. It also helps with managing fatigue while getting in and out of tight spaces like tents, sleeping bags, and bunks.

With the ranger crawl exercise, it is important to engage the core, arm, and shoulder muscles prior to beginning the movements. Starting in the plank position, swing your right knee out and forward towards your right elbow. Lightly tap your toes on the ground a foot to the right of your body and as far forward as possible. As you're doing this, keep your hips low to maintain a straight back, as in the plank position. Pause, and then return your right leg to the start. Now swing the left knee out and forward towards your left elbow, and tap the ground about a foot to the left of your body, as far forward as possible. Pause, and return your left leg to the start position. Repeat 10 times.

Figure 11.1

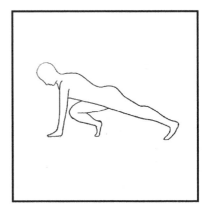

Figure 11.2

Figure 11.3

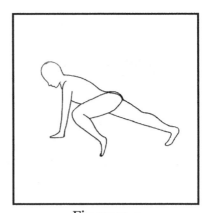

Figure 11.4

Figure 11.5

12. 8-POINT BODY BUILDERS

This exercise is what you get when you ask a Navy Seal to combine a push-up, scissors, a squat thrust, a squat, and a power jump all in one! The benefit of the 8-point body builder is that it is an all-body workout in itself. Not only does it train virtually every muscle in the body, but performing more than 5 repetitions is challenging. When done at the end of the Rainier Dozen, it not only has physiological benefits, but it will also force most people out of their comfort zones. No small amount of mental fortitude is required to complete a set of 10. This exercise is definitely a good candidate for starting at a smaller number and working your way up from there!

Starting in the standing position, drop into a crouch on the ground and then thrust both legs back to the plank position. Perform a push-up. After completing the upward motion of the push-up, jump your legs about 4 feet apart, into "scissors." Return your legs back together so that you are in the plank position again. From here, jump the feet forward into the same crouch position as earlier. Finally, perform a power jump by launching yourself straight up into the air, landing back down into the start position. For a little extra self-motivation or to wake up the neighbors, perform a handclap while in the air during your power jump!

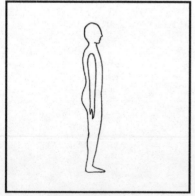

Figure 12.1

Figure 12.2

Figure 12.3

Figure 12.4

Figure 12.5

Figure 12.6

Figure 12.7

Figure 12.8

Figure 12.9

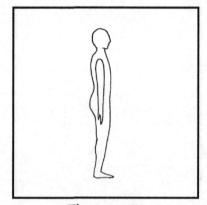

Figure 12.10

SUMMARY

Completing just one of some of these exercises is no small feat, so as noted earlier in this chapter, it is definitely good to start with a small number and work your way up to 10 over the course of a few weeks. If some of the exercises are difficult for you with the prescribed form, it is better to do fewer of them with the right form and work your way up from there. Good form will allow you to gain the benefits of the exercise without injury risks as well as give you a consistent benchmark to measure your improvement as the weeks pass. You can also use some of the given modifications such as widening the stance of your feet in push-ups, while still maintaining good overall form for your body.

SECTION 3

SUPPORT FOR SUCCESSFUL TRAINING

CHAPTER 5
NUTRITION:
FUEL FOR THE JOURNEY

Given the long days and the vast amounts of energy expended, nutrition is an important subject in mountaineering. For the purposes of the *Fit to Climb* training program, I'll look at two major considerations in this chapter: nutrition for training and nutrition for the summit climb. I'll provide a brief overview of fundamental nutrition requirements, followed by examples of challenges unique to the mountain environment. I'll also talk about some practical solutions and tips that I have found to be effective.

Experiment with different quantities and kinds of foods to find what works for you during your training. An important goal of training is to figure out how certain foods react with your body while performing strenuous activities. It almost goes without saying that you shouldn't try something new and exotic during a summit climb! Consult a qualified sports nutrition expert or dietitian as appropriate.

NUTRITION FOR TRAINING

The goal for the training period is to eat in a way that supports your health, recovery from exercise, and athletic improvement. Your food intake should be balanced; stay away from diets that ignore entire food groups. Nutrient-dense foods from all food groups should be key components of your nutrition plan.

The following are 5 key priorities for your nutrition strategy during training:

- High level of nutrient density
- Sufficient carbohydrates and fats to provide energy
- Sufficient protein to support overall body maintenance as well as to improve muscle strength
- Sufficient salts to maintain optimal electrolyte balance
- Hydration

I'll discuss each of these in turn.

HIGH LEVEL OF NUTRIENT DENSITY

Whole and fresh foods, such as vegetables, fruits, nuts, and whole grains, are generally rich in nutrients necessary for maintenance of good health. Many packaged foods, processed foods, and "junk" foods contain energy in the form of fats and carbohydrates, but they are lacking in nutrients such as vitamins, minerals, acids, enzymes, and proteins. For an athlete to eat too many "empty" calories is to miss an opportunity to replenish energy and nutrients that advance fitness gains. High performance machines need high performance fuel. Endurance athletes are no different.

Eat plenty of fresh vegetables during training. Many vegetables can be eaten without cooking, and this is a great way to retain as much of the nutrient content as possible. Vegetables provide important vitamins, minerals, and other phytonutrients critical to health and athletic performance. Your training will be strenuous, and it is critical to keep high levels of nutrients in your system for optimal performance and recovery. Aim for a variety of vegetables to cover a broad range of phytonutrients. Fruits, nuts, legumes, and whole grains are also important, nutrient-dense dietary staples during training.

Sufficient Carbohydrates and Fats for Energy

As training volume and intensity increases, the need for energy increases, as well. This requires that you eat sufficient amounts of carbohydrates to provide your muscles with the necessary glycogen to fuel your activity. Insufficient carbohydrates will lead to poor recovery, painful muscle fatigue, and conversion of valuable muscle protein into energy. There will be times where you might run short of fuel during a training session, but those instances should be the exception and not the rule. Good examples are whole grains, potatoes, sweet potatoes, fruit, and pasta.

Healthy fats are critical to a nutritious diet, and this is especially true for endurance athletes. A diet very low in fat will fall short of providing balanced energy stores. Besides imparting flavor and helping you produce enzymes, which make you feel satiated, fats are energy dense. Fats are generally digested more slowly than carbohydrates and proteins, thus providing energy over a longer period of time. Olive oil, avocados, fish, nuts, and nut butters are examples of nutritious fats.

Sufficient Protein to Support Overall Body Maintenance and to Improve Muscle Strength

Protein is primarily needed to rebuild muscles that have been broken down by exercise. As the body recovers after the stress due to training, providing the right fuel for recovery is a critical part of increasing your fitness level over time.

Protein requirements vary, depending on many factors including body mass, volume, and intensity of training. The recommended daily amount of protein for endurance athletes is equal to 1.8 grams of protein per kilogram of body weight. Once you do the math, you may find that this is often challenging to achieve. Quality sources of low-fat protein include: chicken and other lean meats, seafood, egg whites, soy, low-fat cheese, yoghurt, low-fat milk, and beans (legumes).

SUFFICIENT SALTS TO MAINTAIN OPTIMAL ELECTROLYTE BALANCE

Due to the exertion in training, especially some of the longer sessions, endurance athletes lose sodium through perspiration, evaporation, and urination. Maintaining the right electrolyte balance is very important for endurance athletes, because in order to get better, you actually need to perform well during training. If you're putting out a tremendous amount of effort but are doing so at a diminished capacity, the result may well be a lack of improvement or even a decline in conditioning. For some of the longer training sessions, prepare for the training session like you would prepare for a goal event such as a road race or a summit hike. Eat snacks or foods high in salt such as pretzels or salted trail mix during your training session. Consider replacing part of your water intake with a sports drink such as Gatorade or other equivalent. You may want to approach this cautiously at first by diluting Gatorade with water, as it has a lot of salt and sugar in it already. For very long and intense sessions, consider putting a Nuun tablet or equivalent electrolyte mixture in your water.

HYDRATION

Water is essential to health. Dehydration causes many health problems, reduces performance during workouts, and prolongs recovery from exercise. Particularly on days with hard workouts, by the time you feel thirsty, you are already getting dehydrated, and it might not be possible to catch up. Think of your day as a road trip in your car; you don't wait until you run out of fuel to fill up; you shouldn't do this with your body either.

Try to get ahead of your water intake by starting early in the day with a large glass of water. Throughout the day, stop to drink water at regular intervals. An hour or so before a hard workout, pre-hydrate by drinking a glass of water. Take a sip periodically from a water bottle during all workouts if possible, and certainly the longer and more difficult ones.

As sports science evolves, there is ongoing discussion about how much fluid is necessary. Recommended amounts of fluid intake vary greatly and also depend on a multitude of factors including fitness level, environmental factors, intensity of exercise, and respiration rate. You want to avoid extremes: dehydration on one end and hyponatremia (dilution of sodium levels in your blood due to excess water intake) on the other. A central goal of training is to learn how much fluid you need to avoid being thirsty and to optimize performance. Particularly for some of the longer training hikes, you may want to use the information regarding hydration in the second half of this chapter as a guide, and adjust your approach based on the distance.

NUTRITION FOR THE CLIMB

The goal of managing your nutrition for the climb is to maintain fuel levels that allow you to keep going, stay warm, and mitigate the risk of altitude sickness. The following are 6 key priorities for your nutrition strategy during the actual summit climb, as well as for the longer, harder, training hikes. Some of the following priorities overlap with each other, which is okay.

- Selection of foods high in energy and easily digestible
- Hydration
- Adequate intake of salts (especially sodium)
- Foods to avoid
- Selection of foods that are enjoyable and palatable
- Selection of foods that are easy to carry on the trail

SELECTION OF FOODS HIGH IN ENERGY

Sufficient energy is a key success component in fueling for the climb. Mountain climbing athletes expend more energy than even long-distance cyclists, runners, and triathletes. This is not to say that these sports are not tremendously hard in their own right but to say that the caloric demands of mountain climbing are extreme. Not only are the days long, in some cases involving a high level of physical activity for all the waking hours, but the physical activity takes place in an environment that is harsh and that places significant demands on your fuel systems. Specifically, you will experience cold temperatures, which require that you use massive amounts of energy to stay warm. You will also experience extreme heat, which will cause depletion of fluids, salts, and energy.

Whatever you eat, you must have food that is high in energy. Breads, pastas, rice, cereal, and potatoes are good examples. I recommend packing a selection of vegetables along for their vitamins, minerals, water content, and taste, but these are always in addition to the high energy starches that are essential to maintaining energy.

As part of the strategy of eating foods high in energy, some climbers may choose to "carb-load." Carbohydrate loading is a bit of a controversial topic, so exercise your own judgment in whether you choose this path or not, and consult an expert. The goal of carbohydrate loading is to make sure you start the climb with as much glycogen stored in your muscles as you can. You will burn so much energy on the climb that you won't be able to replenish it all on the mountain. You'll want to eat a carbohydrate rich diet for the 5 days preceding the climb, while at the same time you cut back (taper) your training.

Note that carbohydrate loading is not an excuse to eat without care. Cookies, chocolate, pizza, and pastries are high in carbohydrates and fat but are not nutrient dense. These might help you roll down the mountain but will not help you climb up! Potatoes are high in energy and provide some good protein and nutrients. Roast some baby potatoes with salt and herbs to make a delicious and high-energy meal. Rice, couscous, pasta, oatmeal, bananas, bread, fruit, and fruit juices are all good options as well.

HYDRATION

There are several factors during the climb that create an exceptional requirement for fluid intake: the constant effort, the temperature, and the dry air. Hiking on the lower part of the mountain in summer can invite warm temperatures when combined with direct sunlight, so expect to lose a lot of fluid through sweating. Climbing at night on the upper part of the mountain will cause fluid loss through evaporation. Cold weather increases your respiration rate, and you lose more fluid due to evaporation from respiration.

Humidity is also a factor. Humidity is not directly affected by altitude. However, humidity is affected by air density and temperature. At high altitudes, the air is thinner (lower pressure) and, with a few exceptions, the temperature is lower. At low temperatures and low pressures, air cannot hold as much water vapor. Thus, the humidity is necessarily low when the air is thin and cold.

All of these factors combine to cause dehydration. Avoiding dehydration requires a near constant awareness and a good strategy. I recommend that you drink no fewer that 5 liters of fluid per day when you are on the mountain. My personal method for this is to drink 1 liter within an hour of waking, 2 liters during the climb, 1 during the hour after climbing, and 1 in the evening. It requires a discipline and a method of remembering to do this. Beware of falling behind: it is nearly impossible to catch up during the climb, and you need to start each day hydrated. During the summit climb nearly everyone will experience some level of dehydration. Being aware of this and having a plan in place will help you reduce the risk of dehydration occurring to you.

Most mountain leaders will insist on bottles being inside a pack for safety; you don't want to lose a bottle. Not only do you need that fluid, but a falling bottle is a missile, no less dangerous than throwing a rock down the mountain. Additionally, bottles will freeze if left on the outside of the pack.

I enjoy using hydration packs for many outdoor activities, yet I do not use them on summit climbs for 3 reasons. One, they can get damaged by an ice tool, by a rock, or in a stumble. This could soak your stored clothing. Second, even the insulated tubes or the nozzle can freeze solid, making drinking impossible. Finally, it's tough to ration water in a hydration pack. Some packs have a meter, but with most, it's hard to tell how much is left. I like to know exactly what my resources are, and this is a lot easier with a bottle. Some people do use hydration packs successfully, so consider this a personal choice, or rely on the leaders of your climb team to make this decision for you.

Fortunately, you typically will not have to carry all of this water with you. If you are hiking with a guide service, your guides will help you purify water on the mountain. In the unlikely event that I find water above 10,000 feet, I'll help myself to an extra drink. There are several ways to purify water. Using a filtration device is a useful method, using water purification tablets is another, and boiling water kills all germs. The risk of drinking water from streams or snow is that bacteria from animals or humans will cause gastrointestinal illness during or after the climb. Your guide service will advise you about their preferred method for water purification. It is my opinion that when a climber gets sick on a climb, it is more likely the result of poor personal hygiene. Two things to pay attention to are hand washing before eating, and not eating another person's food. If someone else fails to wash their hands and then puts their hands in a bag of food, bacteria can be transmitted to you if you reach into that food bag. Don't let people put their hands in your food bag. If you want to share, it's best to pour the contents from the Ziploc bag or container into someone's hand.

Adequate Intake of Salts (Especially Sodium)

You lose salts through perspiration and urination. Both of these functions are increased during the climb because of the effort, and because the body regulates your pH balance by lowering water content in order to lower acidity. The low oxygen environment increases acidity.

Eating snacks and foods high in salt will help. I also recommend an electrolyte replacement drink and salt tablets just in case. Sports drinks fall into two categories: with or without added sugar. High energy drinks such as Gatorade have good value on climbs as they provide needed fuel. However, I also enjoy having some no-sugar-added drinks such as Nuun, or similar products. An added benefit of electrolyte tablets like Nuun is that they come in a water-resistant tube, and are therefore light and easy to dispense. On high-output days during both training and climbing, I'll add a Nuun tablet to a sports drink.

The two salts you need to replenish are sodium and potassium, with sodium being a higher priority. The amounts of sodium that need to be replenished vary greatly between individuals and is affected by heat and cold as well as by the intensity and duration of the climb. Experiment during training to find what works for you. My personal choice on summit day is to carry two 1-liter bottles, one with Gatorade and a Nuun tablet, and the other with 3 Nuun tablets and water. I'll also carry an extra tablet or two.

The drug Acetazolamide (sold under the brand name Diamox)—which is commonly used for altitude sickness—is a diuretic, meaning that it promotes the production of urine. Therefore, climbers using it will need to take in additional water and salts in order to compensate.

AVOIDANCE OF FOODS THAT ARE DIFFICULT TO DIGEST

It's natural to think it would be a good idea to eat the way the commercial guides eat on the mountain. However, a commercial guide spends so much time at high altitude that they are more efficient and require less food due to lower energy output. They are acclimatized to the thin air, and their digestive system can handle more stress than most people. As someone who is not accustomed to this environment, there are a couple of things to consider. One, digestion requires oxygen, as does your brain and the rest of your body's systems. If you are nearing your capacity and it's as much as you can do to maintain brain function and cardiovascular output, your body will prioritize these functions and either eject the contents of the stomach or create digestive issues. Two, it's not uncommon for people to experience anxiety during climbs, which can be exacerbated by hypoxia (lack of oxygen). Both these factors can lead to digestive problems.

The body's need for energy is so great during climbs that the last thing you want to do is deprive yourself of nutrients for any reason. Therefore, I recommend that you eat foods that are:

- Easily digestible.
- Flavorful but not overly spicy: Bland foods might not appeal but hot spices may irritate the stomach.

- High in water content: Foods like soup, pasta, and vegetables are good candidates.

- Low in fat: Carbohydrates are the most efficient form of fuel, while fat and protein require more oxygen to digest than carbohydrates.

- Foods you have practiced with and eaten while training.

- Balanced: A mix of simple and complex carbohydrates will be easier to digest and provide more evenly-delivered energy (fewer highs and lows).

SELECTION OF FOODS THAT ARE ENJOYABLE AND PALATABLE

Given the lack of appetite that most people experience at high-altitude, it is important to take foods that will actually be appealing. Personally, I enjoy Mediterranean, some Mexican, and some Asian foods. I'll also often carry herbs, some oil and balsamic vinegar, and sometimes curry powder. On the mountain, I'll use this to season pasta dishes, or I'll just dip bread in it. Pay attention during your training and note which foods you enjoy, which you tolerate, and which you will at least consider eating during extreme efforts. These are the foods you need to select for the actual climb.

CHOICE OF FOODS THAT ARE EASY TO CARRY AND TRANSPORT:

On a summit climb, I put most of my food in the pockets of the down parka I will wear at breaks. I'll usually stash some food in my trouser pockets, too, in case I end up stopped somewhere between breaks. I don't like energy bars much, but they are waterproof and have good wrappers, so I have a few with me. I carry some dried fruit in Ziploc bags. Use the tougher Ziploc bags such as the freezer-bag variety, as they are less likely to tear.

WHAT I CARRY WITH ME

Now that I've talked about all of the different priorities for nutrition for your climb, you're probably wondering how to combine all of those needs into one list of foods to carry with you. Your guide service will give you guidelines on how much food to carry for the climb. Some guide services provide breakfast and dinner, and some services will provide water only. Sometimes this includes hot water, which can be added to dehydrated meals, if that is your choice.

In this section, I'm going to share what works for me. There are two things I think about concerning nutrition for the climb: what to eat and how to organize it. Prior to mountain climbing, I was a competitive cyclist, and I learned how to calculate the energy content of virtually any food because it was necessary to be able to win. This experience has been tremendously useful in mountain climbing, both personally and when I've guided teams of climbers. I highly recommend that you take some time to learn what you can about sports nutrition, because sometimes the difference between success and failure in any endurance sport, especially mountaineering, is dependent on making sure you have enough of the right kind of fuel in the tank. Alternately, find someone with a similar experience and approach, and copy what they do.

Using a formula such as 200 to 300 calories per hour, I calculate how much food I need to carry with me. For me, that is about 5,000 calories total. Note that experienced mountain guides expend less energy than most on these climbs, so make sure you figure out what's right for you, using your guide service's recommendation for help. To portion this out throughout the climb, I figure out how many breaks I'm going to have on each day of the hike. There are normally 5 or 6 breaks on the approach hike to Camp Muir, and 8 breaks on the summit climb and descent. Consult with your guide service to find what is applicable to you. One of the key determinants of how much to eat is how much I can actually ingest. I'm not trying to match my total energy output; I'm just trying to constantly top off my fuel tank. I'll plan on eating at each break and do a quick sanity-check of my food at the end of packing to make sure I have enough for all those breaks.

I organize my food into two 1-gallon Ziploc bags, labeled "TODAY" and "RESERVE." You want today's food easily accessible, because you don't want to waste time on the mountain. If you have a 15-minute break, you really don't want to spend 5 minutes of that time looking for your sandwich. During a break, I will have my pack off, warm jacket on, and will be sitting down, eating and drinking in 60 seconds or less. The more rote you can make this process, the better your chances of success, because you will have increased your recovery time during each break. Practice these techniques during your longer training hikes.

I put as much food as I think I'll need for that day in the TODAY bag, and you should do the same. The RESERVE bag is your food for the remainder of the climb. Put the TODAY bag near the top of your pack so you can get it easily. The RESERVE bag can go anywhere in your pack that optimizes the distribution of load.

I divide my food into sweet, savory, and plain when I put them in the TODAY bag. I have cravings for all three of these, and it's hard to predict when each of these will occur, so it helps to have them quickly accessible.

These are my favorites for the approach hike:

- A foot-long Subway veggie sandwich cut into two (for two rest breaks).
- A Tupperware container with the previous night's leftovers (rice or pasta are favorites).
- 2 bananas
- 2 apples
- Dried fruit
- Nuts
- Smoothie drink (I like Odwalla green superfood)
- 1 can of Pepsi
- A bag of Tim's Honey Mustard potato chips

For the summit hike, I carry the following:

- 4 Lara bars or another energy bar
- A peanut butter and jelly sandwich
- Gu shot blocks
- Trail mix
- Dried mango slices
- A bagel and Swiss cheese sandwich in a Ziploc bag (so it doesn't get smashed)
- 1 liter of Gatorade with 1 Nuun tablet
- 1 liter of water with 3 Nuun tablets

For the descent from Muir to Paradise, I take along:

- A salty snack like a bag of chips, pretzels, or trail mix
- 2 energy bars
- 1 liter of water

CHAPTER 6
EQUIPMENT

In this chapter, I will present you with information about the various pieces of gear that you will need to successfully train, starting with the 10 essentials, and ending with how to organize all of it in your backpack. Individual tastes will vary significantly regarding equipment, and newer versions of items are released by outdoor gear manufacturers every year. Therefore, it doesn't make sense for me to give many specific suggestions. Consult a good outdoor gear store for the latest equipment that fits your budget. I will not talk about the equipment you will need on your summit climb, as this book is intended for climbers with a guide service, and they will provide you with an exhaustive list of what you will need.

I've always thought of equipment selection as a fun part of the adventure. Anytime you are in a remote area away from cell phone reception, the support of emergency services, and the comforts of civilization, it is prudent to have the right equipment. Gear should contribute to safety, efficiency, and comfort, in that order. As an example, a rain jacket should first be able to keep the rain out, as well as be durable enough to survive the rigors of the mountain. In terms of efficiency, while still being effective and durable, it would be nice if the jacket is light, to contribute as little as possible to overall pack weight. Finally, the jacket should be comfortable; otherwise, it will affect attitude and morale.

Renting gear from your guide service is a great option, and very budget-friendly. For instance, for around $30, you can rent a clean and excellent 3-glove system, which will serve you very well on your climb. Buying each of these separately might well cost you upwards of $300, and you may not use them very often.

EQUIPMENT FOR TRAINING

Based on the safety-efficiency-comfort selection process mentioned above, the following list will provide examples of all the equipment you will need for this training program, up until the climb.

Some of the following items are optional on shorter hikes, but use good judgment of your own hiking ability, always hike in groups, and be aware of weather and trail conditions before starting a hike.

10 ESSENTIALS

Here are the 10 essential items that you will want on any hike, no matter the distance. Not all of these items are gear, but the list is a good checklist to go through on any hike. Note that if you are hiking in a group and plan to stick together while on the trail, then some of the items can be shared, to lighten your collective load.

1. A map of the area you are hiking
2. A compass or GPS receiver
3. Protection from the sun: sunglasses and sunblock
4. Extra food
5. Extra water
6. Extra clothes

7. A headlamp or a flashlight

8. A first aid kit

9. Firestarter (matches, chemical heat tabs, canned heat, or a magnesium stick)

10. A knife

I recommend hiking in groups as much as possible. Besides the camaraderie, accountability, and shared motivation, being with someone that can support you is critical if something goes wrong. If this is not possible and you are hiking in unfamiliar territory, I would strongly recommend carrying a whistle to help you signal your position should you need help.

Exhaustive List

Here is an exhaustive list of all the items that you could possibly need on a hike. You probably won't need all of these on every hike, so check weather and trail conditions before you start hiking, in order to be well prepared but not be carrying unnecessary pack-weight beyond the amount your training schedule calls for. Many of these items are self-explanatory, but I've added some details to help you make an informed choice.

FOOTWEAR

Good boots are probably the single most important item to get right for hiking. You will spend the entire duration of the hike on your feet and will pass through varied terrain. The comfort, quality, weather-resistance, and type of boot you use will make the biggest difference between a sanguine experience and a miserable one!

Taking care of your feet is fundamental to completing this training program. If people have foot problems, they will not be able to continue. It's essential to have a well-fitting pair of good quality boots. A good pair of hiking boots may be a significant investment, but it is a very important purchase. One reason to spend a bit more on a pair of boots is that they will last longer if you plan to do a lot of hiking and backpacking.

Here are three boots each, for men and women, that are perfect for northern hemisphere training.

Men's boots:

- Asolo TPS 520 GV Evo hiking boots - Men's
- Vasque Breeze 2.0 Mid GTX hiking boots - Men's
- Zamberlan Vioz GT hiking boots - Men's

Women's boots:

- Ahnu Montara hiking boots - Women's
- Asolo TPS 520 GV Evo hiking boots - Women's
- Lowa Renegade GTX Mid hiking boots - Women's

The kind of boot that you will need for the training is a general hiking boot. A general hiking boot has a medium-weight leather or technical fabric construction and is moderately stiff. Mountaineering boots, in contrast, are extremely stiff, to be used with crampons. They are also insulated to be able to cope with the demands of extreme cold. You will need mountaineering boots for your summit climb, so work with your guide service to figure out the right kind for your trip.

Other footwear-related items you'll need are:

- Hiking socks
- Liner socks
- Foot powder
- Blister prevention tape
- Moleskin
- Superfeet or other brand of insoles
- Spare laces

SAFETY AND SELF-CARE ITEMS

- Crampons
- Lip cream

- Sunblock
- Sunglasses
- Snow goggles (optional, depending on location)

CLOTHING

- Gaiters
- Long underwear (optional, depending on location)
- Hiking pants
- Rain-proof pants
- Regular underwear
- Short-sleeved t-shirt
- Long-sleeved t-shirt
- Fleece or other kind of insulating jacket
- Rain jacket
- Down parka (optional, depending on location)
- Liner gloves
- Mid-weight gloves
- Heavy gloves
- Neck gaiter
- Hat
- Baseball hat or sun hat

OTHER ITEMS YOU MAY NEED

- Maps and trail guides
- Parking passes, if applicable
- National Park Service or State Park entry passes
- Hiking poles
- GPS
- Watch

- Heart rate monitor (optional)
- Notebook and pen
- Emergency contact information
- Safety plan

When getting started, many people have budgetary and time constraints, which make it difficult to purchase everything all at once. What I have found useful is to get the most important stuff as soon as you can. In my opinion, the first priorities are a good pair of boots for training hikes, followed by a backpack. This can be a daypack for training, or you may want to start off the process training with the same pack you'll use on the mountain. Another suggestion is to cross-reference this list with the list of items provided by the guide service you will be using for the climb, and buy items that you will be able to use during your training as well as your expedition. Lastly, keep in mind that while you don't need to buy equipment with a lot of bells and whistles, you should invest in quality gear for the most critical items, such as boots, a backpack, socks, a jacket, hiking pants, and sunglasses.

How to Organize Your Backpack

Putting some thought into organizing your backpack will pay dividends on your training hike, and especially on your mountain expedition. On your climb, expending excess energy digging through your pack during rest breaks, or worse, being unable to find a critical item, can significantly impact your likelihood of success as well as your sense of calm. In addition, having a well-balanced pack will make each step you take as comfortable as can be.

REI has an excellent article on how to pack your backpack, and there are many other good resources on the web. There is no perfect way to pack every backpack, so try out different options during your training, and see what works for you.

https://www.rei.com/learn/expert-advice/loading-backpack.html

The basic idea is to consider items that you will need at different times and with different frequencies on your hike, as well as the weight of certain items, and place them in your pack accordingly. Items that you will need only at the summit should be at the bottom of the pack, while items that you will need at every rest break should be at the top of your pack or in easily accessible pockets. Heavier items should be towards the middle of the pack to give you a balanced load. Your pack should be laterally balanced (similar weight from left to right). You may even consider writing down on a piece of paper the items that are in each enclosure of your backpack, so that you can quickly determine where an item is, should you forget.

Organize your food into separate, labeled Ziploc bags based on when you will be eating them. This will allow you to take small amounts of food out and keep them in your jacket pocket for quick access. I have found that freezer bags tend to be tougher than regular Ziploc bags, and I use them when climbing for an extra bit of safety against food spillage.

Your individual pack may have some specific instructions with it, and in that case, please follow those instructions for optimal packing. In general, about 70% of your weight should be supported by your hips and about 30% by your shoulders. If the pack is the correct size for your body, you'll have the waist belt fitting comfortably on the hips. If you place your thumb just above the waist belt of your pack, you should be able to touch your iliac crest (the small bone that sticks out on the side of your hip). If the waist belt is too high, chances are your pack is too short and you'll end up carrying too much weight on your shoulders. This will lead to unnecessary fatigue.

Over the course of your training program, on your long hikes, you will carry a pack weighing between 15 pounds in week 6 and 45 pounds in week 14. There are a couple of ways to manage the weight of your pack. If you have more weight than you need or want to carry in that particular week, then a way to shave off small amounts of weight is to get rid of cases for some items and wrap them in clothes or jackets instead. You can also save space within your pack, and make your pack more compact in general, by nesting items within one another where possible. If you are hiking with friends, you can also share some items.

If, on the other hand, your pack is lighter than the desired weight for that week of training, then you can use extra clothes or gear that you have been collecting for your climb to add some weight. This has the added benefit of allowing you to test out equipment well before you need them in a critical situation on the mountain. If you don't have the specific items that you're climbing with yet, you can carry extra food or water. Water is a particular good choice as you can discard it at the turn-around point and lessen the strain on your knees as you descend.

MAINTAINING YOUR EQUIPMENT

Before every training hike and your expedition, it would be wise to go over your equipment and make sure that everything is in good working order. This might include checking or replacing batteries and replacing items in your first-aid kit if you used them the last time you were out on the trail. Waterproof items, such as jackets, gaiters, gloves, and hiking pants, might need treatment with products such as Nikwax to retain their correct operation when you need it most. In fact, water-proofing might be best undertaken after each training hike rather than just before the next one, as it can take a few hours. Check your boots to see that they are not damaged, the laces aren't frayed, and that they are clean and dry. Replace socks that might have holes in them, and replenish any consumable items such as sunblock or lip balm.

A NOTE ABOUT EQUIPMENT FOR THE CLIMB

Besides the equipment you'll use during your 16-week training period, there are additional items you will need when you summit Mount Rainier, such as ropes or a climbing helmet. This book is intended for the mountain athlete who will be climbing with a guide service, and all the popular guide services in the Seattle area have a comprehensive list of all the gear you will need, including clothing, footwear, safety gear, and climbing-specific equipment. Additionally, your guides will spend a good amount of time telling you about this specialized equipment you will need and training you to use these items safely and correctly. This orientation is included as part of the climb package. Lastly, depending on the guide service, you may not have to carry certain items up the mountain yourself. These will be provided for you at the mountain hut at Camp Muir. As a result, I won't talk about those items here. Discuss this with your guide service, and rest assured that you will be in the safest hands possible!

While I am on the topic of gear, here is a quick note about your training program and how the recommended pack weights fit in. As noted above, if you are planning to climb with a guide service, then you will likely not need to carry certain items in your pack. As a result, the weight of the pack that you will be carrying will be about 45 pounds, depending on the exact weight of your backpack, clothing and other items. The training program recommends a progression of pack weights on your endurance hikes that will target this final weight. It starts at 15 pounds in week 6 and ramps up gradually to 45 pounds by week 12.

If you are climbing independently or are with a community-based organization such as the Mountaineers, that provides training but doesn't provide guided expeditions, then you may have to carry some of these items in your backpack. Depending on the size of your group, you may choose to share certain items, such as tents, and spread the weight across your group. In my experience, independent climbers will need to carry about 55 pounds per person in their packs. If this is your plan, adjust the weights for the hikes to ramp up steadily from 15-20 pounds in week 6 to 55 pounds in week 12, in increments of 5 or 10 pounds per week.

CHAPTER 7
SELF-CARE AND RECOVERY

You cannot fight the mountain. If you try, it will win.

—Unknown.

It is the same with the training process. Self-care throughout the training program and on the mountain climb, itself, will help you summit successfully. The focus of this chapter is about taking care of your body as you are working hard through your training as well as on the summit climb.

The *Fit to Climb* program emphasizes moderation and consistency. The "no pain no gain" philosophy will not help your training success nor will it keep you safe on the mountain. There will be times during training to go all-out. However, these times will be during specifically identified peak training sessions. The hard efforts will be balanced with a foundation of moderate and consistent effort that builds steadily towards a goal of success on summit day.

Recovery is also critical to your success: you must recover before you build back up. By going too hard without proper recovery, you will get lesser results than by going too easy. In this chapter, I discuss self-care during training and on the mountain climb to aid in that recovery. Included in this chapter are also some suggestions for stretching as well as important strategies on the mountain to practice during training.

While you may not expect illness or injury, they do occur. This 16-week program allows for time and leeway for when you need additional rest due to illness and injury. You can adapt and improvise if correct training and recovery methods are adhered to throughout the program.

SELF-CARE DURING TRAINING

RECOVERY AND OVERTRAINING

While a full discussion of training theory is beyond the scope of this book, I've included a brief explanation here to help you consider the danger of over-training. For more information, an excellent resource is the book *Periodization: Theory and Methodology of Training,* by Tudor Bompa. The author is regarded as the father of periodization training, a well-established underpinning of endurance sports.

When you apply a stimulus to your body, whether through aerobic, anaerobic, or strength training, the body goes into a state of fatigue. If you allow some time for the body to recover, this fatigue dissipates, and the body returns to the baseline state you were in before that training session. However, the body then temporarily exceeds the previous baseline state, in a manner proportional to the intensity of the stimulus applied. This excess above your previous baseline state is called over-compensation or super-compensation.

If the intensity of training you perform is just right or a bit on the low side, then in either case the body will accumulate some gains in level of fitness before the next stimulus (your next workout) is applied. Over time, this will result in a raising of your baseline level of fitness. If you take it too easy, you may see only small gains in your level of fitness, but you will not degrade your fitness level. These two cases (training hard or training too easily) can be seen in the first two parts of the picture on the next page.

However, if you train too hard, or do not allow for the appropriate quality or amount of recovery time, your body will not have the time to recover to the previous level of fitness equilibrium. In this state, applying a new stimulus (your next workout) results in the body starting a new cycle of fatigue-recovery-overcompensation from a position of fitness-debt. Over time, this will result in a general degradation of your fitness level. This can be seen in the third part of the picture on the next page.

Specifically, overtraining results in reduced performance, fatigue, and often psychological effects such as depression, reduced enthusiasm, and poor sleep and appetite. Quality sleep and nutrition are important factors in recovery. Overtraining will not only have a significant direct impact on your training progress but can actually turn into a downward spiral from which it is difficult to escape.

Signs of overtraining can include persistent muscle soreness and fatigue, increased resting heart rate, increased tendency towards illness, and poor quality of sleep. If you think you are overtraining, consult a physician, cut back on the intensity and length of workouts, re-assess your nutrition strategy, particularly your protein intake, and make sure you get plenty of sleep. Waking up an hour earlier to put in more effort, whether in fitness or your career, is not a good long-term strategy and will backfire in the end.

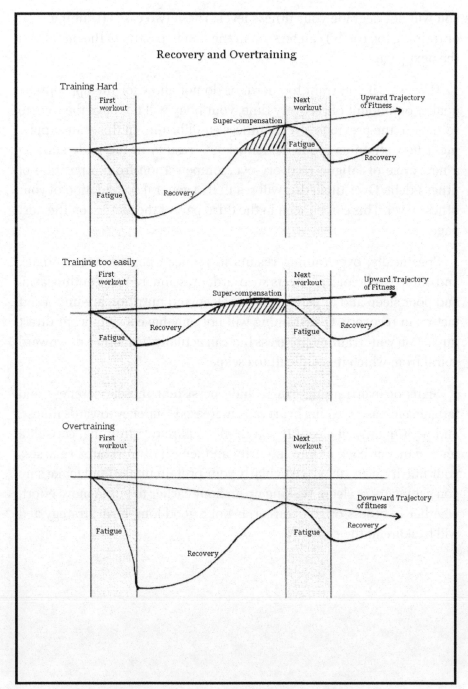

Figure 13.1: Recovery and Overtraining

Resolving Fatigue

This training program isn't easy, and there is no doubt that you will experience fatigue after some workouts. Having said that, it is important to learn to distinguish between when you are lacking motivation and when you are severely fatigued. While this diagnosis will be different for each athlete, the following are some basic tips to recognize the signs of fatigue and address them.

- As an overall comment, pay attention to how your body feels right after all workouts and on the day following hard workouts. Learn your limits and adjust your training if necessary.

- Remember that the training program as a whole and the climb are primarily about measured, consistent effort. While there are instances during the training (the high-intensity workouts) where you will need to make an effort well above your baseline, these are included in a planned manner and timed so as to allow for recovery. During aerobic training sessions, try to focus on a measured, consistent output of energy.

- Stay hydrated and fuel yourself properly. Proper nutrition, before, during (the longer workouts), and after, will result in long-term success.

- Warm up before training sessions, or you may impede your ability to complete the workout as intended. A proper warm-up takes about 5 to 10 minutes, consists of aerobic activity of low to moderate intensity, and warms up your muscles by a few degrees.

- Extreme fatigue resulting in dizziness or vomiting should be avoided completely.

Nutrition

Proper nutrition supports both performance and recovery, so do not cheat yourself by improperly fueling your body. You need ample nutrients and calories to train well. Eat nutrient dense food and hydrate sufficiently. There is no question that you will burn ample calories during this training program, and refueling with delicious, nutrient dense food, not empty calories, is important to the training program. Severe restriction diets will likely not be helpful; you are shorting yourself the nutrients and calories needed to complete the workout. If appropriate to your case, consult a specialist in sports nutrition or a physician. A detailed discussion of nutrition needs for the mountain athlete is in the chapter titled "Nutrition: Fuel for the Journey."

REST, RESTORATION, AND RELAXATION

Incorporate some alternative therapies and activities into your routine to optimize your fitness program. Restoration is key to continuing to make progress and improvement with your fitness. Find the balance that optimizes your training as well as your attitude toward training. Address both physical and mental aspects of restoration. The techniques below have worked well for me during my training.

I have found meditation to be useful to finding some balance in an already-busy life into which I am introducing a vigorous training program. There are many ways to meditate, and I don't believe that there is one right approach. Personally, I have found that simply sitting quietly for as few as 5 minutes before a workout brings me to a state of increased focus and calm during the workout.

Proper rest will achieve greater results than overtraining. Rest days are structured in the program and should be used. Recovery walks can be quite restorative and will promote fitness after a strenuous workout and between workouts. Sleep is critical to muscles recovering from strenuous workouts. Most adults need 7 to 9 hours of sleep for good health. Give yourself adequate sleep to recover and grow stronger.

Massage can help ease sore muscles and possibly help prevent injuries. Consider seeing a massage therapist who specializes in sport injuries. Any nagging pains can be addressed by a physical therapist. This is not a good time to ignore any pain or persistent discomfort.

Lastly, but perhaps most importantly, training often takes time away from family and friends, unless you are lucky enough to be able to share this experience with some of them. Be sure to incorporate time into your schedule to relax with family and friends to help restore the balance of near constant focus on training and work.

Injury Awareness and Prevention

The training program is designed to ease into a progression of strength and aerobic training and thereby prevent injuries. However, if you are hurt at any point, back off the intensity, slow down, and assess how you feel. If you experience a sharp pain, stop to address it right away and seek medical attention. Particularly on your hikes, if you feel a hot-spot indicating that a blister is forming, stop right away and apply moleskin. Do not try to "gut it out." It will have a negative impact on your training schedule. Minor injuries and soreness can be eased by ice baths and the "RICE" technique (Rest, Ice, Compression, and Elevation).

Stretching

Treatises have been written on stretching, and I will not repeat all of them here. Stretching is a vital but often ignored part of a workout, as we rush off to work or other commitments. Stretching after a workout helps to reduce muscle fatigue and soreness, improve blood circulation, and improve flexibility and mobility.

Consider ending every workout with a cool-down walk and some stretching. At a minimum, choose stretches that will work on your back, hamstrings, quadriceps, and torso. There are 4 stretches listed below, but I encourage everyone to add stretches that you feel comfortable doing to their repertoire. Include stretches that might address any particular problem areas that you have. Some good resources are the authoritative *Stretching: 30th Anniversary Edition* by Bob and Jean Anderson or the "Home Stretch" section in the book *Fit by Nature: The Adventx Twelve-Week Outdoor Fitness Program* by yours truly.

In the same way that you may have found a regular time of the day to perform the Rainier Dozen exercises, perform some of these stretches at the end of the day. In addition, consider stretching periodically throughout the day, like a cat. I think we tend to underestimate the good it will do and only think it important right after a workout.

TWISTERS

Stand with legs shoulder-width apart and arms straight out to the sides, with your palms facing upward. Keep hips facing forward, and twist your upper body to the right, such that your left arm is in front of you and the right arm behind you; that is, a 90-degree rotation. Pause here for a second, and then twist the other way until your left arm is behind you and your right arm in front of you. This is not a stretch to do with speed but rather to feel the stretch with each turn. Don't skip the pause for a second at the apex of the stretch on each side. Pay attention to how your back and shoulder muscles respond.

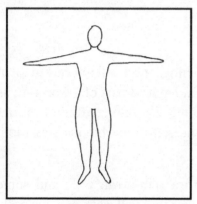

Figure 14.1

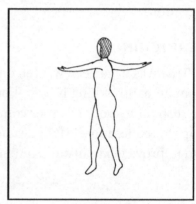

Figure 14.2

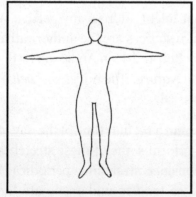

Figure 14.3

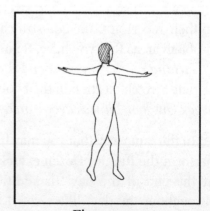

Figure 14.4

BACK STRETCHES

Lie on your back with knees bent and feet on the ground. Stretch your arms out on the ground to form a "T" with your torso. Keeping your shoulders firmly on the ground, move your knees to the left until they touch the ground (if possible), or as far as you can go. Turn your head in the opposite direction. Hold for 20 seconds, and repeat on the other side.

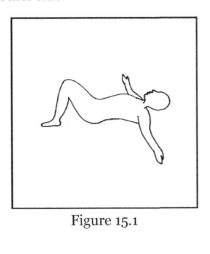

Figure 15.1

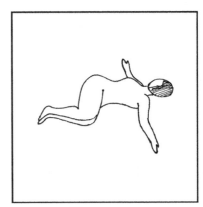

Figure 15.2

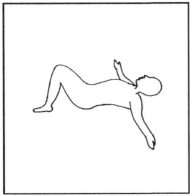

Figure 15.3

Figure 15.4

HAMSTRINGS

Lie on your back with legs straight on the ground. Raise your right leg as far as possible, while maintaining a slight bend in your right knee. This is to isolate the hamstrings for this stretch. Grasp the raised leg with both hands below the knee (around the lower thigh), and pull gently toward the center of your body until you feel the stretch. Try to straighten out your raised knee if possible as you do so, but do not lower your leg. Hold for 20 seconds, and repeat with the other leg.

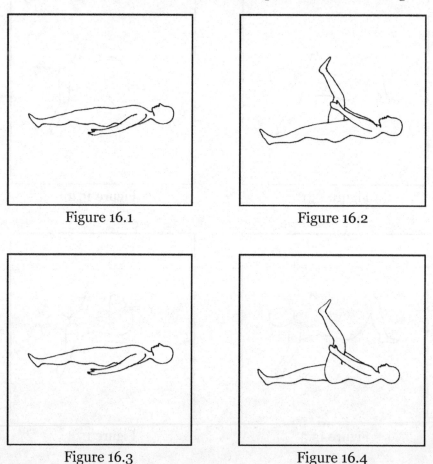

Figure 16.1

Figure 16.2

Figure 16.3

Figure 16.4

QUADRICEPS

Start in a standing position, and hold onto a support (such as a tree or a park bench) with one hand if needed. Grasp your left ankle with your left hand, and gently pull the ankle toward the back of your body. Try to stay as upright as possible, with your chest open, hips straight, and the knee of your raised leg pointing downwards. Don't let your knee drift outwards from your body. Hold for 20 seconds, and repeat on the other side.

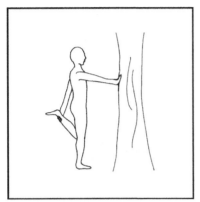

Figure 17.1	Figure 17.2

WALKING

We often underestimate the power of walking to offer an opportunity for both stretching and recovery and to continue to build a base of fitness. Consider making opportunities to increase your walking throughout the day. Get off the bus a few stops early. Park farther away from where you need to go. Add a lunchtime stroll, or consider taking a walk during small-group meetings. We spend a lot of time sitting, and walking will do wonders to stretch out sore and tired muscles, while gently adding greater fitness.

CHALLENGE BY CHOICE

In my personal coaching practice, I use the concept of Challenge by Choice. The idea is to put in the hands of my clients the choice of how far to push themselves. On any given day during your training, there may be a variety of factors that contribute to how you feel, whether physically or mentally. You may choose to take a day off or make the workout a little easier than planned, or you may choose to push hard because you're feeling great. You can apply this logic to any of the workouts; whether by starting with 3 daily push-ups in the Rainier Dozen and working your way up to 10, or by going for the higher end of the recommended hike distance if you feel up to it and are well prepared. Some discomfort is okay during training, but pain is never a good thing. Practice being self-aware of the signs your body is giving you, and adjust your effort accordingly.

As you take on the adventure that is this training program, the Challenge by Choice mantra applies to the big picture just as it does to each workout. Plan rest and relaxation days in your training, as well as time to connect with other aspects of your life, such as friends, family, hobbies, travel, work commitments, or other interests.

SELF-CARE FOR THE CLIMB

Proper preparation prevents poor performance.

—British Army

The majority of self-care on the mountain is driven by organization and habits that are practiced in training. The goal is for self-care actions to become second nature. Depending on your location and altitude, some of these items may not have been a factor during training, but you will want to consider them during the climb.

SKIN CARE

Between the sun, cold, and dry air, your skin will take a beating on the mountain. Preventing problems before they occur is critical, so use sunblock and use it often. There are different kinds of sunblock, and the best kind is the one that you are likely to use often. Figure out what works for you during your training, and use that. Most climbers will want to use a sunblock rated at SPF 30 or higher.

Foot Care

Considering that you will be spending the better part of 14 hours on your feet, the best thing you can do to take care of your feet is to get yourself boots that fit well, keep you warm, and are well suited to the terrain that you will be traversing. Make sure that you have socks that work well with these boots, and consider carrying an extra pair of socks so that you can switch to a fresh pair at some point during your climb. Similar to your training, take care of any blisters that crop up as early as possible by applying moleskin.

Eye Care

A bright, sunny day on the mountain can make for enjoyable climbing conditions, but you will want to take care that your eyes are protected from snow blindness. Use a baseball hat at a minimum at the lower altitudes, and once you leave Camp Muir, it is important to use sunglasses. Large polycarbonate lenses, in a style that fits close to your face, are ideal to minimize your exposure to bright sunlight. Anti-fogging lenses, or the use of an anti-fog lens cleaner, will also reduce the need for you to stop and tend to your glasses should they fog up due to your warm breath.

High-Altitude Ailments

The summit of Mount Rainier is at an altitude of 14,411 feet, and every year, some climbers are impacted by different kinds of high-altitude ailments. The most common symptoms are headaches, dizziness, shortness of breath while exerting oneself, nausea, decreased appetite, and difficulty sleeping. If you believe that you might be susceptible to altitude ailments or have experienced them on other climbs, it may make sense to take certain precautions to minimize the chance of a negative impact on your Mount Rainier expedition.

There are various ways of limiting the impact of altitude ailments, but before I discuss them, I want to emphasize that it is critical that you communicate with your guide about your symptoms and how you are feeling. High-altitude ailments can be deadly in some circumstances and for some individuals; so, communicating with the guides will allow them to make the safest possible decision for the group, including descending to a safe altitude, if appropriate. It would also be useful to discuss this concern with your guide service while signing up for your trip.

Planning for an extra day or two to acclimatize to high altitude is one of the best ways to address altitude ailments before they become a major problem. Consider the different options that your guide service might have available; for instance, a 5-day climb might allow for an extra day at Camp Muir to adjust to the altitude as well as to enjoy the stunning views of the glaciers from there. Depending on how far you will travel to climb Mount Rainier, you may also work in an extra day after you land to rest before heading towards the mountain to begin your expedition. If you are local to the Seattle or Portland areas, or any area that has access to an elevation over 10,000 feet, then plan one of your long hikes to Camp Muir or to a mountain where you live. This will give you a good sense of your ability to deal with high-altitude ailments. Being physically fit, the central goal of this book, will give you a good chance of being resilient to such ailments, though they will not prevent their occurrence. Lastly, this content is not intended to be an exhaustive and authoritative medical guide to high-altitude ailments, so please conduct some research and consult an expert, such as a physician who is familiar with the demands of high altitude and who may be able to provide medication.

POSITIVE PRESSURE EXHALATIONS

Positive pressure exhalations, or pressure breathing, are one of the best techniques to counteract the lower atmospheric pressure at high altitudes. The idea is to breathe as deeply as possible, from your belly, which results in taking in more oxygen than breathing through your chest. It also expels more carbon dioxide, thus slowing muscle fatigue.

To practice this technique in a controlled environment, start by lying on your back. You can put your hands on your stomach to help visualize the effect of your deep breaths. Breathe in as deeply as possible, visualizing your hands (or belly) pushing as high towards the ceiling as possible. Hold this breath in for a second; then, purse your lips and breathe out forcefully, visualizing your hands (or belly) dropping towards the floor. Hold for a second or two, and then repeat. When you feel like you have the hang of this method in a state of rest, try incorporating it into your training hikes to get some more practice with it.

On the mountain, you can apply the same technique. If and when you start to feel any shortness of breath, use the pressure breath as described above for a short while, such as 30 seconds or a minute. Take some time to breathe normally, and repeat the sequence a few more times as necessary.

Maintaining a Steady Pace and the Rest Step

If you find yourself exerting too much energy, slowing your pace down a bit so as not to approach your anaerobic threshold is a good idea. Start out at a slow and steady pace after each rest break until you hit a stride that you can comfortably maintain.

Another technique that experienced hikers use to take pressure off their muscles and conserve energy is called the rest step. This tool also has the natural effect of slowing your cadence. It transfers the pressure you would normally feel in your muscles to your body's bone structure.

From a standing position, lock the knee of one leg, and keep all the weight of your body on that leg. Swing your other leg forward and up the mountain. You can stop in this position, with your weight on the knee of your rear leg, and your front leg relaxed on the incline, for as long as necessary. When you're ready to move forward, move your weight forward onto the front knee, step forward with the other leg, and lock the new rear knee. Repeat this process, alternating resting and locking each leg, until you feel like you can switch back to a normal gait.

Hydration and Nutrition

Use your training hikes as an opportunity to practice with different kinds of food and liquids. This will allow you to develop a good idea of how much you need to consume per hour on your expedition. While on the mountain, the important thing is to keep ahead of your hydration and nutrition goals. Drink consistently, and do so before you get thirsty. A good way to gauge that you are keeping up with your hydration needs is by making sure that your urine is colorless. Also, make a plan and eat regularly at each rest break, even if you don't particularly feel like it at that time. Keep some high-carbohydrate snacks handy so that you have ready access to them on the mountain without having to stop and dig into your backpack.

Putting It All Together: The Ideal Rest Break

During each of your rest breaks, you will want to take care of many of the above self-care activities. In addition, you may want to adjust your clothing by adding or removing layers, take a quick bathroom break, attend to a potential blister on your foot, or simply take a mental break to re-focus yourself. All of these activities together can easily add up, so it's important to make efficient use of your time during these breaks.

Practice rest breaks during your training so you can repeat the same behaviors seamlessly on the mountain. Time yourself using a stopwatch so that you know what to expect. Multi-tasking is a good strategy; you can eat and drink while you are adjusting your clothing between bites. Having a checklist of things to assess or accomplish at each rest break can also help to keep you on track and moving along without dawdling. Rest breaks on guided expeditions are typically 10 to 15 minutes, so if you can get all of your activities down to a just a few minutes, you will have a few minutes to devote to rest, both mentally and physically.

SECTION 4

THE TRAINING PROGRAM

CHAPTER 8
OVERVIEW OF THE TRAINING PROGRAM

I've broken up this 16-week training program into 4 phases. The concept of periodization is a well-established protocol for endurance sports, and I want you to establish yourself at each level of the training, while continually getting closer to the levels of fitness you will need to climb Mount Rainier. In this introduction to the training program, you will also find some tips about how to plan out your training for each type of workout. I've also included an overview of the entire training program in one place, for easy reference.

The 4 phases of the *Fit to Climb* training program are:

ADAPTATION PHASE (2 WEEKS)

You'll spend this phase learning and getting accustomed to the exercises. You'll have some leeway for missing sessions, but getting into a good rhythm early will set you up for greater success later. You'll learn some key concepts that you'll practice for each of the 16 weeks. You'll get out on a trail and get started with an easy hike.

FOUNDATION PHASE (7 WEEKS)

The main goal of this phase is to establish a base for the rest of your training program and your climb. You'll perform aerobic, anaerobic, and strength training, with some workouts targeted at those individual competencies as well as some workouts that improve different facets of your mountain-fitness at once. You'll start adding some weight to your pack towards the end of this phase. The length of your hikes will increase gradually over the course of this phase. By the end of this part of your journey, you'll have sufficient levels of core and leg strength for the climb.

PEAK PHASE (5 WEEKS)

Just as you'll need to raise your game as you get closer to the summit on your climb, you'll take your fitness to a very high level in this phase of the training. This phase is primarily about extending your endurance. Missed sessions or neglect of recovery and self-care will have consequences on your performance; you'll want to be diligent about taking care of yourself. These 5 weeks are critical to your success on the mountain. Besides the physical fitness you'll gain, the ease with which you handle your endurance hikes will give you the confidence to take everything the mountain throws at you during your climb.

EXPEDITION PHASE (2 WEEKS)

You'll scale back your training to conserve energy for your climb. You'll prepare both mentally and physically for the climb. You'll organize all your equipment and make any last-minute preparations needed. You'll maintain your hard-won levels of fitness by mixing in workouts and hikes of the intensity of approximately week 8, and you'll mix in a few judicious rest days.

PLANNING YOUR WORKOUT PROGRAM

As you get into each week of the training program, I have included more detailed descriptions of each workout when they are first introduced. Having said that, there are some things you can do at the outset to set yourself up for success with each kind of workout.

HIKES

The cornerstone workout of this training program is undoubtedly the long hike on day 7 of most weeks. The long hike is designed to build aerobic endurance. Depending on where you live, you may or may not have access to a lot of mountainous terrain. Doing some research about hikes that are within a reasonable driving distance or finding alternate options such as urban parks or hilly areas within your city or town will pay dividends when you get to your hiking days.

The *Fit to Climb* training program is designed to include elevation gains on your long hikes. For the Adaptation phase, the goal is simply to get boots on the trail, get accustomed to aerobic exercise, and figure out logistics. Therefore, don't worry too much about the elevation involved. If it is possible to get out on a mountain trail, so much the better. For the Foundation phase, I have not suggested any elevation-gain targets for your hikes, but aiming for 500 feet per mile of ascent is a good guide. As an example, for your 7 to 8-mile hike in week 8 (4 miles ascending and 4 miles descending), you may aim for 2,000 feet between the starting point and the summit or turnaround point.

For the Peak phase, you will ramp your training into high gear, and this is certainly true of the endurance hikes. On some hikes, you will recreate efforts that are close to those you will experience on your summit adventure. As a result, I have made some recommendations for elevation-gain targets. These aren't meant to be overly prescriptive, and it is perfectly acceptable to trade off some distance for elevation gain if you are unable to find such a location. For the final phase, you will scale back your training in preparation for your expedition, so use your body and mind as a guide; simply do what feels good to you.

I have also made recommendations for getting used to pack weights, ramping up from 15 pounds in week 6 to 45 pounds in week 12, and holding it at that level through the end of the Peak phase. This 45-pound target is based on the amount that guided climbers typically carry, but your pack weight might vary somewhat depending on the exact gear that you are carrying. For instance, certain down jackets might weigh more or less than others for the degree of insulation that they provide. If you know the exact weight of all the gear that you will be taking on your final expedition, feel free to adjust this weight target for your own needs. See the "Equipment" chapter for a note on how much weight to use in training if you are climbing independently.

Lastly, refer again to the "Equipment" chapter for a reminder on the 10 essentials as well as additional items that you should carry with you on hikes. For the first few weeks, the hikes are relatively short and you may never be more than an hour away from a parking lot. However, as the lengths of the hikes increase, try to hike in groups if possible for additional safety. It's a good idea to let someone know where you will be and when you expect to get back to civilization.

STAIR WORKOUTS

The stair workouts in this book aim to build up your aerobic and anaerobic fitness by raising your anaerobic threshold. If you are fortunate to have access to outdoor stairs that allow you to go up them for 3 minutes near where you live, then I would recommend using them. If not, using the stairwell of an office or apartment building or a machine like a Stairmaster or stepper at the gym are good substitutes. Seattle-based athletes are fortunate enough to have access to an astounding 650 sets of public stairs. Search the web for "public stairs in [your area]" to see what is available where you live.

STRENGTH TRAINING

The third aspect of the 3-pronged approach to mountain fitness is strength training. There are two types of fitness activities in this training program that will develop your strength: the daily Rainier Dozen exercises and strength-focused workouts. I am a big proponent of outdoor fitness adventures, and as such, none of the strength workouts in this book require any equipment other than park benches for triceps dips, a grassy area for steam engines on your back, and perhaps 20 yards of open space for shuttle runs.

For the Rainier Dozen workout, your biggest task might be finding a time of the day when you can do the exercises. I like to do them first thing in the morning, as this pays dividends throughout the day in the form of a slightly elevated metabolic rate and greater alertness. However, any time of the day works. Since you are trying to build a habit, I recommend picking a time of the day that works daily. For the harder exercises, I would also suggest that you start from a lower number of repetitions and work your way up to the number suggested.

CROSS-TRAINING

The idea of the cross-training workout on day 6 of most weeks is to stay active with some moderate exercise, engage different muscles than you might be using on the other days of the week, and have fun! Consider exploring a new sport or physical activity, or try different things each week for even more variety. A game of soccer, a yoga session, or a bike ride on a nice day are all excellent options. I am sure you can find something that suits you.

REST AND RECOVERY

The training program has rest and recovery days built in. During most weeks, days 3 and 5 are rest days, and the easy hike on day 1 is meant to be a recovery workout. Listen to your body and don't overtrain. I highly recommend investing some time in learning some new stretches and undertaking other mental and physical self-care activities. An occasional sports massage can do wonders after a particularly hard workout or difficult week. Consult a physician or physical therapist if you experience any pain.

QUICK VIEW OF THE ENTIRE TRAINING PROGRAM

ADAPTATION PHASE

WEEK	DAY 1	DAY 2	DAY 3	DAY 4	DAY 5	DAY 6	DAY 7
1	Rainier Dozen	Hike (30m)	Rainier Dozen / Rest	Hike (30m)	Rainier Dozen / Rest	Hike (1h)	Rainier Dozen
2	Rainier Dozen	Hike (40m)	Rainier Dozen / Rest	Hike (40m)	Rainier Dozen / Rest	Hike (2h)	Rainier Dozen + Rest

FOUNDATION PHASE

WEEK	DAY 1	DAY 2	DAY 3	DAY 4	DAY 5	DAY 6	DAY 7
3	Hike (30m)	Stairs (40m)	Rainier Dozen / Rest	Strength Circuit x 2	Rainier Dozen / Rest	Cross-Training (1h)	Hike (2h, 4 miles)
4	Hike (30m)	Stairs (40m)	Rainier Dozen / Rest	Strength Circuit x 2	Rainier Dozen / Rest	Fitness Test	Hike (2h, 4 miles)
5	Hike (30m)	Stairs (50m)	Rainier Dozen / Rest	Strength Circuit x 3	Rainier Dozen / Rest	Cross-Training (1h)	Hike (3h, 5-6 miles)
6	Hike (30m)	High-Intensity Stairs x 4	Rainier Dozen / Rest	Strength Circuit x 3	Rainier Dozen / Rest	Cross-Training (1h)	Hike (3h, 5-6 miles, 15 lb)
7	Hike (30m)	High-Intensity Stairs x 5	Rainier Dozen / Rest	Strength Circuit x 4	Rainier Dozen / Rest	Cross-Training (1h)	Hike (3h30m, 6-7 miles, 20 lb)
8	Hike (30m)	High-Intensity Stairs x 6	Rainier Dozen / Rest	Strength Circuit x 4	Rainier Dozen / Rest	Fitness Test	Hike (4h, 7-8 miles, 25 lb)
9	Hike (30m)	High-Intensity Stairs x 7	Rainier Dozen / Rest	Strength Circuit x 4	Rainier Dozen / Rest	Cross-Training (1h)	Hike (5h, 9-10 miles, 35 lb)

PEAK PHASE

WEEK	DAY 1	DAY 2	DAY 3	DAY 4	DAY 5	DAY 6	DAY 7
10	Hike (30m)	1-2-3 Stairs x 3	Rainier Dozen / Rest	High-Intensity Stairs x 7	Rainier Dozen / Rest	Cross-Training (1h)	Hike (5h, 9-10 miles, 35 lb, 2,500 ft)
11	Hike (30m)	1-2-3 Stairs x 4	Rainier Dozen / Rest	High-Intensity Stairs x 8	Rainier Dozen / Rest	Cross-Training (1h)	Hike (7h, 12-14 miles, 40 lb, 3,500 ft)
12	Hike (30m)	1-2-3 Stairs x 4	Rainier Dozen / Rest	Fartlek Hike (1h30m)	Rainier Dozen / Rest	Hike (3h, 5-6 miles, 30 lb)	Hike (7h, 12-14 miles, 45 lb, 3,500 ft)
13	Hike (30m)	1-2-3 Stairs x 5	Rainier Dozen / Rest	Fartlek Hike (1h45m)	Rainier Dozen / Rest	Hike (3h, 5-6 miles, 30 lb)	Hike (9h, 15-18 miles, 45 lb, 4,000 ft)
14	Hike (30m)	1-2-3 Stairs x 5	Rainier Dozen / Rest	Fartlek Hike (2h) / High-Intensity Stairs x 8-10	Hike (2h, 3-4 miles, 1,500 ft)	Hike (4h, 7-8 miles, 45 lb, 2,500 ft)	Hike (7h, 12-14 miles, 45 lb, 4,500 ft)

EXPEDITION PHASE

WEEK	DAY 1	DAY 2	DAY 3	DAY 4	DAY 5	DAY 6	DAY 7
15	Hike (30m)	Stairs (1h)	Rainier Dozen / Rest	Stairs (1h)	Rainier Dozen / Rest	Equipment / Food Prep	Hike (4h, 7-8 miles, 35 lb)
16	Hike (30m)	Stairs (30m)	Rest / Travel	Orientation	Mountain Training	Climb to Camp Muir (6h)	Adjust to altitude + Hike (2h)
	Summit Climb (14h)						

Tables 1.1 - 1.4: Quick View of the Training Program

CHAPTER 9

ADAPTATION PHASE

PULSE CHECK

This is the first training phase of your Mount Rainier adventure. Much like buttoning up a coat, it's really important to get the first button in the right hole. Otherwise, no amount of effort at the other end is going to make the process successful! Take time to absorb as much as you can during the Adaptation phase (the first 2 weeks). These 2 weeks aren't hard, so enjoy them—the honeymoon won't last forever. Each week includes a briefing regarding the week ahead, a table that shows you all the workouts, a detailed description of each workout, and a summary of what you learned and experienced during that week.

In physical training, one of the most important foundational principles is to develop correct movement patterns. The *Fit to Climb* method to accomplish this is the Rainier Dozen, which you saw in Section 2. My biggest encouragement for you in the first week of training is not to measure your success by the amount of effort and intensity you put into the workouts, but rather to focus on performing the exercises with the greatest amount of skill possible. Consider what you want to occur when you're on your climb. You may be clambering over large rocks covered in ice, wearing crampons and a heavy backpack. You may potentially be in a snowstorm. At that point, you'll want your foot to end up precisely where you want it to go, and you'll want to have the strength and coordination to efficiently move your body upwards. The very first step toward getting there is to figure out how to move your body right. Therefore, at this stage, do not worry about how many exercises you can do. Simply focus on the quality of movement and set a good trajectory for the weeks and months to follow.

The second focus for this phase is to put some effort into considering the logistics of how your training will work. Simple explorations and decisions about where you will do the workouts, how you'll get there, and considerations of future hikes will give you a sense of organization and confidence about how this program is going to work for you.

WEEK 1

BRIEFING

The primary focus of this week is to apply your learning of the Rainier Dozen, which you read about earlier in the book. Refer to the instructions to make sure that you establish and practice the correct form for these exercises. With any new routine, there will naturally be a learning curve. By repeating the workout every day, you'll find that you know a lot more about how your body moves by the end of this week.

One choice you'll want to make is when to do it. I find that one benefit of doing the Rainier Dozen the first thing in the morning is that you get it out of the way. Another benefit is that it engages all the muscles of your body early in the day. This boosts your basal metabolic rate and aids your movement throughout the day in all of your activities.

The hikes for this week are short: 30 minutes and 1 hour. The key to hiking is to just do it. It is true that there will be a nice benefit to hiking in a realistic mountain setting, on a trail, for instance. However, at this stage, there is no need to over-think where you're going to hike; just go somewhere. I like to hike around a park; some people will hike on a treadmill, or even in a mall. Some people walk at work.

I have designed this week conservatively so that anyone with average fitness can start off on the right foot. Everybody's fitness ability is different. If this routine is significantly less than you normally do on a weekly basis, then the right thing to do is to adapt so that you maintain your current level of activity. One cautionary note on adaptation is that what's important about weeks 1 and 2 is the type of exercise rather than the volume or intensity. Therefore, it's okay to add additional (moderate) workouts onto the Rainier Dozen and the hikes, but you would not want to replace them.

DAY	WORKOUT	TIME & DIFFICULTY
1	Rainier Dozen	12m Medium
2	Rainier Dozen + 30-Minute Hike	42m Medium
3	Rainier Dozen or Rest	12m Recovery
4	Rainier Dozen + 30-Minute Hike	42m Medium
5	Rainier Dozen or Rest	12m Recovery
6	Rainier Dozen + 1-Hour Hike	1h12m Medium
7	Rainier Dozen	12m Recovery
	TOTAL	**3h24m**

Table 2: Week 1 Workout Calendar

DESCRIPTIONS OF WORKOUTS

DAY 1: RAINIER DOZEN

Concentrate on performing the exercises with the greatest skill possible. Try to keep your body in a comfortable position to start, and visualize your core being strong and stable. Don't worry about speed and resistance, or even about completing the full set on every exercise if that is difficult. The goal is to create a habit by doing the exercises every day.

Perform all 12 of the Rainier Dozen exercises. Your *Fit to Climb* adventure has officially begun!

DAYS 2 AND 4: RAINIER DOZEN + 30-MINUTE HIKE

Start your day with the Rainier Dozen, or use the exercise routine as a warm-up before you hike. Either way, continue to concentrate on getting the movements right and just learning the exercises. Follow this up with an easy 30-minute hike.

DAYS 3 AND 5: RAINIER DOZEN OR REST

Begin your day with the Rainier Dozen. It would be good to take a complete rest day, but if you are used to more activity, feel free to engage in another 30 to 60 minutes of light exercise.

DAY 6: RAINIER DOZEN + 1-HOUR HIKE

Perform the Rainier Dozen exercises and spend 1 hour on an easy hike. If you are already in good shape, feel free to make the hike slightly longer, but don't overdo it.

DAY 7: RAINIER DOZEN

Finish off the week with the Rainier Dozen exercises. As you perform each set of these exercises for the seventh time, take the time to review the workouts in the "Rainier Dozen" chapter to make sure you are getting the movements right.

SUMMARY

Congratulations, you've just completed the first week of your training!

WEEK 2

Briefing

You're probably getting quite skilled at the exercises you've been doing. This week's goal is to take that skill to the next level. There is no better time to develop efficient movement patterns than at the start of the process. Look around at any park or gym and you'll see a range of movement skills: some precise, some not so much. 15 weeks from now, your success on Mount Rainier will depend on many things. Precision is one of them. Success or failure can depend on your ability to put your foot right where you want it to go, not two inches one way or the other. Develop this precision in your training early on and it will serve you well—not just for the entire *Fit to Climb* program, but beyond that as well.

In terms of the type and volume of exercise this week, everything is the same as week 1 except the hikes, which increase in duration. You should be getting the hang of the exercises by now, but continue to concentrate on performing them with the best skill you can.

Descriptions of Workouts

DAY 1: RAINIER DOZEN

Perform the Rainier Dozen exercises, and continue to focus on building your skill level while doing so. Prioritize quality over quantity now, and your fitness level will increase over time.

DAYS 2 AND 4: RAINIER DOZEN + 40-MINUTE HIKE

You'll notice that this week the hiking distance increases a little bit. Be creative with your weekly hiking; perhaps consider getting off the bus a few stops earlier or you could walk to a meeting instead of driving. You're probably noticing now that the hike has a mental benefit as well as a physical benefit. Many people report that walking is a wonderful stress reliever and boosts their energy.

DAY	WORKOUT	TIME & DIFFICULTY
1	Rainier Dozen	12m Recovery
2	Rainier Dozen + 40-Minute Hike	52m Medium
3	Rainier Dozen or Rest	12m Recovery
4	Rainier Dozen + 40-Minute Hike	52m Medium
5	Rainier Dozen or Rest	12m Recovery
6	Rainier Dozen + 2-Hour Hike	2h12m Medium
7	Rainier Dozen + Rest	12m Recovery
	TOTAL	**4h44m**

Table 3: Week 2 Workout Calendar

DAYS 3 AND 5: RAINIER DOZEN OR REST

Begin your day with the Rainier Dozen. It would be good to take a complete rest day, but if you are used to more activity, feel free to do another 30 to 60 minutes of light exercise.

DAY 6: RAINIER DOZEN + 2-HOUR HIKE

Before setting out on this hike, take a few moments and skim the chapters on "Equipment" and "Self-Care and Recovery"; make sure you have what you need for your excursion. In terms of the location of the hike, you can choose something interesting, such as a state park or a wilderness area, or you can stay close to home. If you live in a large city, you can have a lot of fun by doing urban hikes. With a little research, you'll find it's easy to create challenging routes, including elevation, stairs, parks, and maybe a break at a coffee shop. The key is spending time on your feet.

DAY 7: RAINIER DOZEN + REST

This is the completion of the Adaptation phase of your training journey. Perform the Rainier Dozen exercises, but otherwise take a complete day of rest.

SUMMARY

Congratulations! You've completed the Rainier Dozen 14 times, which is a total of 168 minutes of exercise. That's nearly 3 hours of high-quality training! You're also already practicing moderation and consistency, two critical factors in athletic success.

CHAPTER 10
FOUNDATION PHASE

Pulse Check

This third week is the start of the Foundation phase. Over the last 2 weeks, you have experienced what it feels like to get your body used to training in a way that will serve you well going forward. Over the course of the 7-week-long Foundation phase, you will incorporate all three kinds of workouts in this training program—aerobic, anaerobic, and strength training. This phase will therefore lay the foundation for your mountain fitness journey.

You've already experienced aerobic workouts such as the short hikes in your first 2 weeks, and you'll continue to hone the skills you've practiced so far. A few things to look forward to are the addition of new workout types: an interval training workout on stairs and a dedicated strength-training workout.

By their very nature, intervals are challenging, and you'll get out of this workout what you put in. However, you should think of interval training as a force-multiplier because repeated high-intensity efforts produce fitness gains at a much greater rate than steady-state training. So, find a way to spark your enthusiasm in the same way that an athlete would focus going into a championship event.

Another way that these short efforts will pay off on the mountain is by giving you a physiological and psychological edge. Should you find yourself needing to make a bold, sustained effort, perhaps in a storm or on a steep section of the climb, you'll know that you have what it takes. For a further detailed description of interval training and its benefits, refer to the chapter "What Type of Training Is Important." I will describe the specific workouts in the weeks ahead.

The other new element in the Foundation phase is a workout focused on strength training. Strength training is the third element of the triangle of aerobic, anaerobic, and strength training. Performing the Rainier Dozen daily for 16 weeks will help you build up core strength gradually. This will provide an overall boost for all your activities in training and on the mountain. The strength workouts in this phase focus on the specific needs of mountain climbing and help you develop the maximal strength necessary to power through obstacles and reach the top of the mountain.

Lastly, you will continue to build your aerobic endurance by extending the lengths of hikes progressively as you work through the Foundation phase. You will start with a 2-hour hike in week 3 and finish with a 5-hour hike in week 9.

WEEK 3

BRIEFING

The purpose of this week's training is to add 2 new workouts into the mix: stair interval training and a dedicated strength-training workout. By now, you're getting used to the long hikes on the weekend, which are primarily targeted towards increasing aerobic endurance.

One new element in this week's training is interval training on stairs. In preparation for this new element, choose a location where you'll be performing this workout. A set of stairs—indoors or outdoors—would be ideal, but you can substitute a stair climber at the gym if you like. Pick a location that allows you to climb for 2 to 3 minutes continuously before turning around and descending.

In weeks 3, 4, and 5, you will be performing the stair workouts at a consistent pace and with a moderate intensity. For most people, this will not reach your anaerobic threshold and therefore isn't anaerobic training. However, if you are doing this workout outside, the very nature of the stairs will result in periods of higher effort (going up), followed by periods of lower effort (coming down), implicitly creating an interval workout. This will get you used to stair workouts, and prepare you for high-intensity interval workouts in the weeks to come.

The strength training circuit is designed to be done anywhere, indoors or outdoors. It's a great workout to do with friends, if you're training in a group. A stopwatch or timer app on your phone will come in handy.

DESCRIPTIONS OF WORKOUTS

DAY 1: RAINIER DOZEN + 30-MINUTE EASY HIKE

By now, you're used to starting off the week with the mountain in mind and the Rainier Dozen getting you energized every morning. Are you starting to notice any differences now that you've got about 14 sessions of the Rainier Dozen under your belt?

The second part of this workout involves hiking. Today's hike is a recovery workout, and you can also substitute it with a different activity, such as running, biking, or swimming. The important thing is to move at a moderate pace for 30 to 45 minutes. A good yardstick is a pace at which you can hold a conversation with your hiking partner. You do not need to be dripping with sweat at the end of the workout.

DAY	WORKOUT	TIME & DIFFICULTY
1	Rainier Dozen + 30-Minute Easy Hike	42m Easy
2	Rainier Dozen + 40 Minutes of Stair Interval Training	52m Medium
3	Rainier Dozen or Rest	12m Recovery
4	Rainier Dozen + Strength Circuit Training x 2	39m Hard
5	Rainier Dozen or Rest	12m Recovery
6	Rainier Dozen + 1 Hour of Cross-Training	1h12m Medium
7	Rainier Dozen + 2-Hour Hike (4 miles)	2h12m Medium
	TOTAL	**6h01m**

Table 4: Week 3 Workout Calendar

DAY 2: RAINIER DOZEN + 40 MINUTES OF STAIR INTERVAL TRAINING

Good luck with your first interval-training workout! Be prepared to sweat. Interval training is challenging, but it's also exhilarating. In preparation for this workout, you'll have chosen your location already. Your goal is to climb at a consistent pace throughout the workout. The last set of stairs should be completed in about the same time as the first set. Therefore, pace yourself. The descent will be easier than the climb up, resulting in natural intervals within the workouts.

Warm up for 10 minutes with some light jogging or the Rainier Dozen. Then, spend 20 to 30 minutes at a consistent pace on the stairs. Spend about 2 to 3 minutes climbing up, before turning and coming down the stairs at the same pace. Make sure to take 5 to 10 minutes to cool down at the end of the workout as well.

DAYS 3 AND 5: RAINIER DOZEN OR REST

Begin your day with the Rainier Dozen. It would be good to take a complete rest day, but if you are used to more activity, feel free to take another 30 to 60 minutes of light exercise.

DAY 4: RAINIER DOZEN + STRENGTH CIRCUIT TRAINING X 2

Circuit training can be done alone or with friends. I think it's more fun with friends! If done in a group, it's handy to write the name of the exercises down on cards. Arrange the cards in a circle and have each person choose where they start. One person can manage a stopwatch: 40 seconds exercise, 20 seconds rest, and rotate. At the end of each exercise, simply move clockwise or counter-clockwise. You know that 1 full set is complete when you get back to the exercise you started with. Take 1 full minute to rest between each set. If you're doing this workout yourself, simply go through the list below at the same cadence.

- Steam engines
- Push-ups
- Three-quarter squats
- Russian twists
- Lunges
- Steam engines lying down
- Mountain climbers
- 8-point body builders

This week, your goal is to do 2 complete sets of these exercises. When you're done, take 10 minutes to cool down by stretching or walking.

DAY 6: RAINIER DOZEN + 1 HOUR OF CROSS-TRAINING

In preparation for the hike tomorrow, you can do whatever you want today, as long as it adds a benefit to your climb training. For instance, yoga, circuit training, cycling, using a Stairmaster, or playing a game of soccer are all valid forms of cross-training. You could mix it up and try a different kind of exercise each week if you have access to these options. It's important that the exercise is vigorous enough to achieve a cardiovascular benefit and that it is different enough to provide a respite from the singularity of your hiking training. Just like with any other workout, make sure to warm up sufficiently. The Rainier Dozen is great for this.

It may seem inconceivable at this point that you would ever get bored of hiking, but in 8 weeks' time, when you enter the peak phase of your training, you'll want your enthusiasm for hiking to remain high. So, I recommend you set the variety in place right away to ensure that the entire training program is enjoyable, successful, and interesting.

DAY 7: RAINIER DOZEN + 2-HOUR HIKE (4 MILES)

Pick a hike in or near your city that would allow you to cover about 4 miles in 2 hours, depending on the terrain and gradient.

A good goal for today is to hike at an even pace. If you're new to hiking, this pace may seem quite slow, but it's important to remember that you're ultimately training your body to be able to hike at this pace for up to 14 hours on summit day.

SUMMARY

The reality of this week is that you're going to be tired at the end of it. The exciting thing is that you've completed the first week of the Foundation phase and you've covered 2 (aerobic and strength) of the 3 kinds of training you will encounter in this program. You now have your boots on the trail, so to speak. While the following weeks will become progressively more challenging, the gains going forward are simply incremental steps based on what you have already achieved. Take a little time to celebrate; you are well on your way to the summit of the mountain.

WEEK 4

If you can't measure it, you can't improve it.

—Peter Drucker

BRIEFING

This week you'll add in an intense workout, the fitness test. The fitness test is a workout you'll repeat towards the end of the Foundation phase, so this is a good point at which to set a baseline.

Testing your fitness from time to time is a great way to gauge improvement and to take the opportunity to find your limits. The fitness test in this book is a custom version of a military fitness test that can be done during a short workout. The test consists of a timed run, followed by a strength test with 4 exercises designed to gauge your upper-body strength, core strength, leg strength, and agility. For the timed run, I suggest a mile. If you don't like to run, then walking is perfect.

Given the intensity of the workout on day 6, this is a good time to review how your body is responding to the training and make sure you are getting plenty of rest and quality nutrition. Take the extra time to stretch out your muscles if they are tired.

DESCRIPTIONS OF WORKOUTS

DAY 1: RAINIER DOZEN + 30-MINUTE EASY HIKE

Perform the Rainier Dozen, and follow it up with approximately 30 minutes of easy hiking. Feel free to mix things up occasionally with a different activity, such as running, biking, or swimming.

DAY 2: RAINIER DOZEN +
40 MINUTES OF STAIR INTERVAL TRAINING

Repeat your stair interval-training workout from last week. Warm up for about 10 minutes, and then climb up and down a set of stairs at a consistent pace for about 20 to 30 minutes. Cool down with some stretching.

DAY	WORKOUT	TIME & DIFFICULTY
1	Rainier Dozen + 30-Minute Easy Hike	42m Easy
2	Rainier Dozen + 40 Minutes of Stair Interval Training	52m Medium
3	Rainier Dozen or Rest	12m Recovery
4	Rainier Dozen + Strength Circuit Training x 2	39m Hard
5	Rainier Dozen or Rest	12m Recovery
6	Rainier Dozen + Fitness Test	1h12m Hard
7	Rainier Dozen + 2-Hour Hike (4 miles)	2h12m Medium
	TOTAL	6h01m

Table 5: Week 4 Workout Calendar

DAYS 3 AND 5: RAINIER DOZEN OR REST

Begin your day with the Rainier Dozen. Feel free to take another 30 to 60 minutes of light exercise if you feel like it (a brisk walk is a great option). It would also be good to take a complete rest day instead. Listen to your body. If you feel tired, rest.

DAY 4: RAINIER DOZEN + STRENGTH CIRCUIT TRAINING X 2

Repeat the strength circuit-training workout introduced last week. After warming up, perform 2 sets of the following exercises. Spend 40 seconds performing the exercises, and take 20 seconds between exercises to rest and rotate. Take a full minute of rest between each set.

- Steam engines
- Push-ups
- Three-quarter squats

- Russian twists
- Lunges
- Steam engines lying down
- Mountain climbers
- 8-point body builders

Take 10 minutes to cool down by stretching after you're done.

DAY 6: RAINIER DOZEN + FITNESS TEST

After a good 10-minute warm-up followed by the Rainier Dozen, first complete the timed run for a distance of 1 mile. Go at a speed that feels like an intense effort but one that you can maintain for the full mile. Record your time. Then, recover for 5 minutes by gently walking or just pacing slowly back and forth.

For the strength test, find an area that has a solid, level, and soft surface. During this test, you will perform 4 exercises for 2 minutes each, with 3 minutes of rest between each exercise. For a reminder on good form for these exercises, refer to the "Rainier Dozen" chapter. For the fourth exercise, the 20-yard shuttle run, you can set up your shuttle run course with some cones or water bottles. If you aren't sure of the measurement, use 25 normal paces as a guide. Run back and forth between your markers for 2 minutes, counting each back-and-forth loop as 1.

For all 4 exercises, the goal is to count the number of perfect repetitions you can complete in 2 minutes. Break the 2 minutes into 30-second mental segments; this will help you maintain a steady pace. If you do the exercises with a partner, you can rest while counting their repetitions—along with providing encouragement! Write down your scores for each test. Perform the strength test by completing the following for 2 minutes each, with 3 minutes of rest in between each exercise.

- Push-ups
- Steam engines lying down
- Three-quarter squats
- 20-yard shuttle run

DAY 7: RAINIER DOZEN + 2-HOUR HIKE (4 MILES)

This week's hike is the same as the last week. Hike at a steady pace at a location that allows you to cover about 4 miles in 2 hours, depending on the terrain and gradient.

SUMMARY

Is the fitness test a hard workout? For most people, it certainly is! Performing an exercise for 2 minutes may not sound like a lot, but your body will know it is working hard! The good thing is that you're taking stock of your progress in a measurable way, and if you follow the workouts in the following weeks, you'll see a tremendous amount of improvement by the next time you perform this fitness test.

For some folks, certain exercises might be very hard at this early stage of the training program. That's okay. Keep doing the Rainier Dozen exercises, and you'll see a gradual but methodical increase in fitness as time progresses.

WEEK 5

Briefing

The purpose of this week is to extend all aspects of your fitness a little bit—by increasing the length of the stair training, the circuit training, and the hike. You'll add 10 minutes to the stair training, but maintain the same even pace throughout the workout. You'll add another set to the strength training on day 4. On day 7, the length of the hike increases to 3 hours. The day of your fitness test reverts back to your choice of cross-training activity.

DAY	WORKOUT	TIME & DIFFICULTY
1	Rainier Dozen + 30-Minute Easy Hike	42m Easy
2	Rainier Dozen + 50 Minutes of Stair Interval Training	1h02m Medium
3	Rainier Dozen or Rest	12m Recovery
4	Rainier Dozen + Strength Circuit Training x 3	48m Hard
5	Rainier Dozen or Rest	12m Recovery
6	Rainier Dozen + 1 Hour of Cross-Training	1h12m Medium
7	Rainier Dozen + 3-Hour Hike (5-6 miles)	3h12m Medium
	TOTAL	7h20m

Table 6: Week 5 Workout Calendar

Descriptions of Workouts

DAY 1: RAINIER DOZEN + 30-MINUTE EASY HIKE

Perform the Rainier Dozen, and follow it up with approximately 30 minutes of easy hiking. Feel free to mix things up occasionally with a different activity, such as running, biking, or swimming.

DAY 2: RAINIER DOZEN +
50 MINUTES OF STAIR INTERVAL TRAINING

Warm up for about 10 minutes, and then climb up and down a set of stairs, at a consistent pace, for about 30 to 40 minutes. Cool down with some stretching.

DAYS 3 AND 5: RAINIER DOZEN OR REST

Begin your day with the Rainier Dozen. Feel free to take another 30 to 60 minutes of light exercise if you feel like it (a brisk walk is a great option). It would also be good to take a complete rest day instead. Listen to your body. If you feel tired, rest.

DAY 4: RAINIER DOZEN + STRENGTH CIRCUIT TRAINING X 3

After warming up, perform 3 sets of the following exercises. Spend 40 seconds performing the exercises, and take 20 seconds between exercises to rest and rotate. Take a full minute of rest between each set.

- Steam engines
- Push-ups
- Three-quarter squats
- Russian twists
- Lunges
- Steam engines lying down
- Mountain climbers
- 8-point body builders

Take 10 minutes to cool down by stretching after you're done.

DAY 6: RAINIER DOZEN + 1 HOUR OF CROSS-TRAINING

Warm up with the Rainier Dozen, and then spend an hour in some moderately vigorous cross-training activity. Listen to your body, and have fun with it.

DAY 7: RAINIER DOZEN + 3-HOUR HIKE (5-6 MILES)

Think of today as your first serious hiking session. The goal of today's hike is to build some endurance. Make sure to get in a good breakfast so that you are well fueled. You may drive to the trailhead, so give yourself a few minutes to get organized before you set off. Hopefully, you've already identified your hike by this point; but if not, pick something in or near your city that would allow you to cover 5 to 6 miles in about 3 hours depending on the terrain and gradient. As before, try to hike at an even pace. For the first mile, hold back a little and walk at a moderate pace to get your body warmed up.

With the gains in efficiency and cardiovascular endurance, this 3-hour hike may not seem much harder than the previous week's hike. By now, you'll be getting used to boots and pack, and enjoying your local hiking spots.

SUMMARY

In many ways, week 5 can be a breakthrough, and it's often reported by climbers that this is the week where they feel a demonstrable increase in their fitness. Often, the thing that people notice is an increased aerobic capacity; you simply can do more without getting out of breath. Some people also report feeling stronger. All of this makes sense. If you've done all the workouts, you'll have logged 25 solid days of training. This amounts to 25 improvement cycles, and as long as you're practicing good self-care, you can't help but feel stronger. I think it's important to acknowledge the progress and perhaps celebrate in some way. You should feel confident about what you're doing. You've made significant gains, and the foundation you're building at this point will result in greater gains still, as the next few weeks unfold.

WEEK 6

Briefing

Last week you bumped up the length of three workouts, and you're probably still a little bit tired. This week, you'll introduce a new workout, a high-intensity interval-training workout on stairs. The goal of this is to kick your anaerobic training into gear, and this will complete the triangle of aerobic, anaerobic, and strength training that makes up this fitness program.

High-intensity training is exactly that, intense. While performing these workouts, you can expect that your muscles will burn as they go into oxygen debt. You are going to be gasping for air and feel your heart pounding in your chest. This workout will be very challenging and will require mental fortitude to complete each effort, especially towards the end of the interval.

During the high-intensity workout, you will be pausing between intervals until your heart rate returns to about 60% of your maximal heart rate. Many fitness watches or stand-alone heart rate monitors provide the ability to measure your heart rate, and they are certainly good tools. A low-tech alternative is also to take your pulse for 15 seconds and multiply by 4. After a couple of weeks, you will find that you don't need to measure your heart rate because you will be able to gauge when you have recovered to about 60% and are ready to go again. I am a big fan of this last approach; it teaches me to listen to my body.

Descriptions of Workouts

DAY 1: RAINIER DOZEN + 30-MINUTE EASY HIKE

Perform the Rainier Dozen, and follow it up with approximately 30 minutes of easy hiking. Feel free to mix things up occasionally with a different activity, such as running, biking, or swimming.

DAY	WORKOUT	TIME & DIFFICULTY
1	Rainier Dozen + 30-Minute Easy Hike	42m Easy
2	Rainier Dozen + High-Intensity Stair Training x 4	45m Hard
3	Rainier Dozen or Rest	12m Recovery
4	Rainier Dozen + Strength Circuit Training x 3	48m Hard
5	Rainier Dozen or Rest	12m Recovery
6	Rainier Dozen + 1 Hour of Cross-Training	1h12m Medium
7	Rainier Dozen + 3-Hour Hike (5-6 miles, 15-pound pack)	3h12m Medium
	TOTAL	7h03m

Table 7: Week 6 Workout Calendar

DAY 2: RAINIER DOZEN + HIGH-INTENSITY STAIR TRAINING X 4

Warm up with the Rainier Dozen for 12 minutes. Then take 10 minutes to warm up on the stairs at a moderate pace, and finish this phase at the bottom of the stairs. Now, you're ready to start your first interval by running up the stairs.

Each interval should ideally be between 30 and 45 seconds long, and can go up to 60 seconds. The interval should be performed at a high intensity, which means it should feel like about 85 to 90% of your maximum ability. The reason to not go 100% is that you want to remain in control. Allow a rest period that is adequate to allow your heart rate to come down to a point that feels like 60% of maximum, about 3 minutes. Once your heart rate is returned to that level, you're ready to go again. Note that depending on the length of the stairs you are climbing, you can rest where you finish an interval or by going down the stairs until you reach the 60% threshold.

Repeat the interval 3 more times for a total of 4 intervals to complete the core portion of your workout. Cool down with some walking and stretching.

Note that the rest portion of intervals is equally as important as the effort part. The decision to make the next effort before reaching the recovery point will result in the training being ineffective. Additionally, it's important to walk away from interval training feeling like you could have done 1 more effort. In other words, don't go at 100% of your maximum ability.

The reason I start with 4 intervals in week 1 and add 1 interval per week is because we're focused on high intensity and high-performance efforts that are designed to increase your anaerobic fitness. The result of adding intervals gradually will be a staggering increase in your performance ability without risking injury through an abrupt transition. As each week goes by, you'll find that the training should not feel any harder because as you add intervals, you're correspondingly increasing your fitness levels to cope with the increased demands on your body.

DAYS 3 AND 5: RAINIER DOZEN OR REST

Begin your day with the Rainier Dozen. Feel free to take another 30 to 60 minutes of light exercise if you feel like it (a brisk walk is a great option). It would also be good to take a complete rest day instead. Listen to your body. If you feel tired, rest.

DAY 4: RAINIER DOZEN + STRENGTH CIRCUIT TRAINING X 3

After warming up, perform 3 sets of the following exercises. Spend 40 seconds performing the exercises, and take 20 seconds between exercises to rest and rotate. Take a full minute of rest between each set.

- Steam engines
- Push-ups
- Three-quarter squats

- Russian twists
- Lunges
- Steam engines lying down
- Mountain climbers
- 8-point body builders

Take 10 minutes to cool down by stretching after you're done.

DAY 6: RAINIER DOZEN + 1 HOUR OF CROSS-TRAINING

Warm up with the Rainier Dozen, and then spend an hour in some moderately vigorous cross-training activity. Listen to your body, and have fun with it.

DAY 7: RAINIER DOZEN +
3-HOUR HIKE (5-6 MILES, 15-POUND PACK)

Warm up with the Rainier Dozen. Hike for about 3 hours, covering 5 to 6 miles in distance. Hike at an even pace.

For this hike, you'll start carrying a certain amount of weight in your pack. The goal is to achieve a progression of pack weight, from 15 pounds in this week to 45 pounds at the peak of the training. This will gradually prepare you for your summit climb, and it also makes sense that you will need more food, water, clothing, and safety items as the distances of the hikes increase.

Most people will already be carrying a pack with some of the essentials like food, clothing, and safety gear. If you haven't been doing so yet, aim to load up your pack with about 15 pounds of gear (including the weight of the pack). If you don't meet that target, adding extra water bottles to your pack is an easy way to bump up the weight for the incline, and you can discard any water at the top that you don't need for the descent.

SUMMARY

As you work hard at your workouts, be diligent about self-care and recovery. You do have leeway as you train. If for any reason you feel exhausted or you feel that you're slipping back, it's often best to take an extra rest day or two. Taking more rest is not a negative. This is not to encourage a lack of discipline but to respect and honor the intuition and self-knowledge that we all have when it comes to understanding when enough is enough. A simple rule that is used in elite athletic coaching circles is that if you have to choose one, it is always better to undertrain than to overtrain.

WEEK 7

BRIEFING

This week, you will load up your pack with another 5 pounds of weight. Your ultimate target weight will be 45 pounds, depending on your individual gear, the kind of trip you are taking, and which guide service you may be using. This week takes you a big step closer to that goal. A side benefit of increasing the amount of gear in your backpack is learning how to pack like a pro! See the "Equipment" chapter for some instructions on how to organize your pack.

Since day 1 of *Fit to Climb*, you've been practicing squats, lunges, and other core exercises that are building your upper and lower body strength. This is a great time to refocus on your technique, especially for squats, as they are a great all-round exercise that will pay significant dividends as you increase the length of your hikes.

You'll add an interval to your high-intensity stair-training workout. The strength workout is twice as long as when you started; you'll be doing 4 sets of the 8 exercises. You'll notice that you are building muscle endurance, indicated by your ability to make repeated efforts with less fatigue. Finally, the long hike increases by a half hour or about a mile.

DESCRIPTIONS OF WORKOUTS

DAY 1: RAINIER DOZEN + 30-MINUTE EASY HIKE

Today's hike is a recovery workout, and you can also substitute it with a different activity, such as running, biking, or swimming. The important thing is to move at a moderate pace for 30 to 45 minutes. You should be able to hold a conversation with a workout partner while hiking, and you do not need to be dripping with sweat at the end of the workout.

DAY	WORKOUT	TIME & DIFFICULTY
1	Rainier Dozen + 30-Minute Easy Hike	42m Easy
2	Rainier Dozen + High-Intensity Stair Training x 5	49m Hard
3	Rainier Dozen or Rest	12m Recovery
4	Rainier Dozen + Strength Circuit Training x 4	57m Hard
5	Rainier Dozen or Rest	12m Recovery
6	Rainier Dozen + 1 Hour of Cross-Training	1h12m Medium
7	Rainier Dozen + 3.5-Hour Hike (6-7 miles, 20-pound pack)	3h42m Medium
	TOTAL	**7h46m**

Table 8: Week 7 Workout Calendar

DAY 2: RAINIER DOZEN + HIGH-INTENSITY STAIR TRAINING X 5

Warm up with the Rainier Dozen for 12 minutes. Then take 10 minutes to warm up on the stairs at a moderate pace. Perform each 30-45 second interval by running hard up the stairs at an effort level that feels like 85 to 90% of your maximal ability. Recover until your heart rate has come down to about 60% of maximum, about 3 minutes. Repeat the interval 4 more times for a total of 5 intervals in the workout. Cool down afterward with some walking or stretching.

DAYS 3 AND 5: RAINIER DOZEN OR REST

Begin your day with the Rainier Dozen. Feel free to take another 30 to 60 minutes of light exercise if you feel like it (a brisk walk is a great option). It would also be good to take a complete rest day instead. Listen to your body. If you feel tired, rest.

DAY 4: RAINIER DOZEN + STRENGTH CIRCUIT TRAINING X 4

After warming up, perform 4 sets of the following exercises. Spend 40 seconds performing the exercises, and take 20 seconds between exercises to rest and rotate. Take a full minute of rest between each set.

- Steam engines
- Push-ups
- Three-quarter squats
- Russian twists
- Lunges
- Steam engines lying down
- Mountain climbers
- 8-point body builders

Take 10 minutes to cool down by stretching after you're done.

DAY 6: RAINIER DOZEN + 1 HOUR OF CROSS-TRAINING

Warm up with the Rainier Dozen, and then spend an hour in some moderately vigorous cross-training activity. Listen to your body, and have fun with it.

DAY 7: RAINIER DOZEN +
3.5-HOUR HIKE (6-7 MILES, 20-POUND PACK)

Carrying a pack with 20 pounds doesn't sound like much, but if you're not used to wearing a pack, it's quite normal to experience some tiredness or muscle-ache, especially in the shoulders. If you feel a sharp pain, you should stop. However, if what you feel is muscle fatigue or an ache, do persevere. Your shoulders will become used to the pack over the next few weeks. Note that the 20 pounds include a weight of about 3 to 4 pounds for a mid-weight pack.

An organizational aspect to this workout is to practice loading up your pack so that the gear is easy to access, weather-proof, and packed in a way that uses your strength efficiently. Nothing wears you down like a lop-sided pack. Also, you want to look cool, not like you are walking up the mountain with a sack of potatoes on your back!

On a practical note, if you have been collecting gear for your climb, you could use it for ballast. If you don't have the specific items that you're climbing with yet, you can be creative by adding heavy items such as water and bags of rice, or even spare clothes. A tip for anyone who is worried about knee pain on the descent, is to use water to achieve the desired weight on the way up, but then to empty some of this weight at the high point of the hike so that you can descend with a lighter load, therefore lessening the strain on your body.

Warm up with the Rainier Dozen. Hike for 6 to 7 miles over 3.5 hours.

SUMMARY

You're nearing the midpoint of your training program. You've done the Rainier Dozen up to 49 times, a total of 7 hours, and you can probably feel the difference. You're completing substantial hikes, and you're sprinting up those stairs.

As you progress through your weeks of training, pay close attention to how you feel during your workouts. This self-awareness can help you know what parts of the fitness triangle (aerobic, anaerobic, and strength training) might need a little extra work. It might also help you realize when you're pushing too hard and need to dial it back a little.

WEEK 8

Briefing

The end of this week represents the halfway mark of your Mount Rainier training journey. A question I often ask myself at this stage is, "If I had to do the climb today, how would it go?" I like to think that once I reach the halfway point, I could give it a strong attempt, and with good conditions and the stars aligned, I'd probably make the summit and back.

This is the mindset that goes with the next few weeks. You have quite some time to go and more fitness gains to achieve in order to arrive at the start of the climb in great shape. However, you should feel confident that you are already more prepared than many people will be on summit day.

To quantify that feeling of preparedness, you'll perform the fitness test again this week. You should see big gains in comparison to week 4, due to the volume and intensity of training you've done since then. For the hike, you will increase the length to 4 hours and increase the pack weight by 5 pounds.

There are several subtle but important things to consider as you increase the length of your hike. One of the biggest ones is energy expenditure. If you are spending 450 to 600 calories per hour while you hike (more in cold temperatures), then you can sneak in a 2-hour hike without much of a second thought, and you'll probably have enough energy to complete it just fine. However, to be successful at maintaining energy throughout a 4-hour hike, you'll want to be diligent in preparation—specifically in nutrition—to make sure you have enough fuel in your body for this amount of time.

You'll also want to start considering carefully what you carry in your day pack. On a 2-hour hike, you may never be more than an hour from the parking lot. In comparison, on a 4-hour hike you are twice as far away at the turnaround point. This creates a consideration for self-responsibility and risk management. You'll want to make sure you have the 10 essentials in your pack (see the "Equipment" chapter) and also have an emergency plan in case a mishap should occur. This includes letting people know where you're going and also hiking with other people so that you have strength in numbers.

DAY	WORKOUT	TIME & DIFFICULTY
1	Rainier Dozen + 30-Minute Easy Hike	42m Easy
2	Rainier Dozen + High-Intensity Stair Training x 6	53m Very Hard
3	Rainier Dozen or Rest	12m Recovery
4	Rainier Dozen + Strength Circuit Training x 4	57m Hard
5	Rainier Dozen or Rest	12m Recovery
6	Rainier Dozen + Fitness Test	1h12m Hard
7	Rainier Dozen + 4-Hour Hike (7-8 miles, 25-pound pack)	4h12m Medium
TOTAL		**8h20m**

Table 9: Week 8 Workout Calendar

DESCRIPTIONS OF WORKOUTS

DAY 1: RAINIER DOZEN + 30-MINUTE EASY HIKE

Today's hike is a recovery workout, and you can also substitute it with a different activity, such as running, biking, or swimming. The important thing is to move at a moderate pace for 30 to 45 minutes. The pace can be conversational, and you do not need to be dripping with sweat at the end of the workout.

DAY 2: RAINIER DOZEN +
HIGH-INTENSITY STAIR TRAINING X 6

Warm up with the Rainier Dozen for 12 minutes. Then take 10 minutes to warm up on the stairs at a moderate pace. Perform each 30-45 second interval by running hard up the stairs at an effort level that feels like 85 to 90% of your maximal ability. Recover until your heart rate has come down to about 60% of maximum, about 3 minutes. Repeat the interval 5 more times for a total of 6 intervals in the workout. Cool down afterward with some walking or stretching.

DAYS 3 AND 5: RAINIER DOZEN OR REST

Begin your day with the Rainier Dozen. Feel free to take another 30 to 60 minutes of light exercise if you feel like it (a brisk walk is a great option). It would also be good to take a complete rest day instead. Listen to your body. If you feel tired, rest.

DAY 4: RAINIER DOZEN + STRENGTH CIRCUIT TRAINING X 4

After warming up, perform 4 sets of the following exercises. Spend 40 seconds performing the exercises, and take 20 seconds between exercises to rest and rotate. Take a full minute of rest between each set.

- Steam engines
- Push-ups
- Three-quarter squats
- Russian twists
- Lunges
- Steam engines lying down
- Mountain climbers
- 8-point body builders

Take 10 minutes to cool down by stretching after you're done.

DAY 6: RAINIER DOZEN + FITNESS TEST

After a good 10-minute warm-up followed by the Rainier Dozen, first do the timed run for a distance of 1 mile, at an intense pace. Record your time and then rest for 5 minutes.

Perform the strength test as follows, counting the number of perfect repetitions you can complete in 2 minutes. Take 3 minutes of rest between each exercise. Write down your scores for each test.

- Push-ups
- Steam engines lying down
- Three-quarter squats
- 20-yard shuttle Run

DAY 7: RAINIER DOZEN +
4-HOUR HIKE (7-8 MILES, 25-POUND PACK)

This week you'll increase the hike duration by a half hour, or approximately a mile. If you are hiking on steep terrain, this could add another 350 to 500 feet in elevation. Adding a half hour may seem like a small increment; but for most athletes, a 4-hour hike will start to feel like a fairly substantial effort. You should be covering about 7 to 8 miles on this hike.

SUMMARY

Congratulations on reaching the halfway point of your training program! Review your performance in the fitness test, and take some time to celebrate your achievements. On the other hand, if things aren't going so well, this is a good time to make a choice: do you want to press on and catch up in the next 6 weeks (through the end of the Peak phase)? Or do you want to step back and refocus on developing a basic level of fitness, before taking things to the next level? This might involve making the hard choice of deciding not to climb this year.

WEEK 9

BRIEFING

This is a big week, as it marks the end of the Foundation phase of your training! The hike will be your longest yet at 5 hours, while day 6 reverts back to cross-training. Your pack weight jumps 10 pounds to 35 pounds. This week's hike should be a confidence builder because you are approaching milestones of distance and weight that are similar to portions of your approach and summit climbs. For climbers on the Disappointment Cleaver route, day 1 on Mount Rainier consists of climbing 4,500 feet in about 5 hours with a 35-pound pack.

DAY	WORKOUT	TIME & DIFFICULTY
1	Rainier Dozen + 30-Minute Easy Hike	42m Medium
2	Rainier Dozen + High-Intensity Stair Training x 7	57m Very Hard
3	Rainier Dozen or Rest	12m Recovery
4	Rainier Dozen + Strength Circuit Training x 4	57m Hard
5	Rainier Dozen or Rest	12m Recovery
6	Rainier Dozen + 1 Hour of Cross-Training	1h12m Medium
7	Rainier Dozen + 5-Hour Hike (9-10 miles, 35-pound pack)	5h12m Medium
TOTAL		**9h24m**

Table 10: Week 9 Workout Calendar

Descriptions of Workouts

DAY 1: RAINIER DOZEN + 30-MINUTE EASY HIKE

Today's hike is a recovery workout, and you can also substitute it with a different activity, such as running, biking, or swimming. The important thing is to move at a moderate pace for 30 to 45 minutes. The pace can be conversational, and you do not need to be dripping with sweat at the end of the workout.

DAY 2: RAINIER DOZEN +
HIGH-INTENSITY STAIR TRAINING X 7

Warm up with the Rainier Dozen for 12 minutes. Then take 10 minutes to warm up on the stairs at a moderate pace. Perform each 30-45 second interval by running hard up the stairs at an effort level that feels like 85 to 90% of your maximal ability. Rest until your heart rate has come down to about 60% of maximum, about 3 minutes. Repeat the interval 6 more times for a total of 7 intervals in the workout. Cool down afterward with some walking or stretching.

DAYS 3 AND 5: RAINIER DOZEN OR REST

Begin your day with the Rainier Dozen. Feel free to take another 30 to 60 minutes of light exercise if you feel like it (a brisk walk is a great option). It would also be good to take a complete rest day instead. Listen to your body. If you feel tired, rest.

DAY 4: RAINIER DOZEN + STRENGTH CIRCUIT TRAINING X 4

After warming up, perform 4 sets of the following exercises. Spend 40 seconds performing the exercises, and take 20 seconds between exercises to rest and rotate. Take a full minute of rest between each set.

- Steam engines
- Push-ups
- Three-quarter squats
- Russian twists
- Lunges

- Steam engines lying down
- Mountain climbers
- 8-point body builders

Take 10 minutes to cool down by stretching after you're done.

DAY 6: RAINIER DOZEN + 1 HOUR OF CROSS-TRAINING

Warm up with the Rainier Dozen, and then spend an hour in some moderately vigorous cross-training activity. Listen to your body, and have fun with it.

DAY 7: RAINIER DOZEN + 5-HOUR HIKE (9-10 MILES, 35-POUND PACK)

Find a location to hike that is about 9 to 10 miles in distance, and takes about 5 hours. Increase your pack weight to about 35 pounds. As always, spend some time in preparation so that you have the right amounts of food, water, clothing, and the 10 essentials with you.

SUMMARY

How do you feel? Compare where you are now with how you felt in week 1. In what ways do you feel different as a result of the endurance, strength, and skills that you've earned?

You are on track to being a strong member of your rope team. This is important because the team leader is always making decisions based on how each person is doing. Your lead guide is constantly making the assessment, "Is this team member an asset or a liability?" She wants to know whether this person can keep going strong for what lies ahead. Going higher always requires the judgment of whether it's a reasonable decision to be ascending massive glaciers on tiny metal spikes, balancing across narrow ladders spanning hundreds-of-feet-deep crevasses tied to your team-mates by a quarter-inch-thin nylon rope.

Individual focus, skill, coordination, and a multitude of factors make up the basis of that judgement; however, physical fitness is the foundation, and you've got it. With the foundation that you have built over the past 9 weeks and with the 7 weeks remaining, you will have what it takes to be an asset. With the fitness that you are continuing to build, you'll earn the trust of your team to go all the way and have the confidence to want to.

Picture yourself climbing in the cool, thin air, more than 2 vertical miles above sea-level, dazzled by sunlight shining out of a cobalt-blue sky. You'll hear nothing but the wind, your breath, the crunch of spikes in the hard snow, and the gentle clink of carabiners as your steps carry you upwards.

7 weeks and you'll be there. Visualize that moment now and when you finish this week's long hike, congratulate yourself on completing the Foundation phase of this training!

CHAPTER 11
PEAK PHASE

Pulse Check

There comes a point in any climb where more than half of the work is behind you. Rather than ease back, you intensify focus but also relax in the knowledge that things are going your way. You are at a similar stage in the training process! Take a moment to reflect on what you've already achieved. The route ahead will be challenging, yet all it asks are incremental gains on the substantial base that you've already built. You are well and truly on your way to a successful summit.

In some ways, the start of a new phase is like the start of a new training program. The goal of this phase is to do 5 progressively more challenging weeks of training at a pace and intensity where you are nudging forward your endurance at a consistent pace.

The hikes over the next 5 weeks are critical to your success on the mountain. They will get progressively harder each week, until in week 14, you are taking on hikes that are similar to the actual climb in terms of volume and intensity of effort. If you weren't paying close enough attention to it before, it is vital that you practice good self-care during this phase.

You won't do any more focused strength-training workouts. You have the levels of strength and muscle endurance to make it on the mountain. Having said that, you'll continue to do the Rainier Dozen every day, and this will maintain your strength conditioning at the level you've achieved.

WEEK 10

Briefing

This week will see the introduction of a new variant of interval training: the 1-2-3 Stair Workout. This workout will push you beyond your anaerobic threshold and help increase both your aerobic and anaerobic capacity over time. The high-intensity stair-training workout that you have been doing on day 2 will move to day 4.

Depending on where you live, you may well be experiencing longer days and brighter evenings, so this will be a chance to get outdoors, perhaps even at the end of the workday. In my estimation, nothing burns workday stress like a stair workout!

The weekend hike will remain the same at 5 hours, or about 9 to 10 miles, and your pack weight will remain the same at 35 pounds. If you were hiking with a lighter pack, this week should give you a buffer to catch up.

Descriptions of Workouts

DAY 1: RAINIER DOZEN + 30-MINUTE EASY HIKE

Today's hike is a recovery workout, and you can also substitute it with a different activity, such as running, biking, or swimming. The important thing is to move at a moderate pace for 30 to 45 minutes. The pace can be conversational, and you do not need to be dripping with sweat at the end of the workout.

DAY 2: RAINIER DOZEN + 1-2-3 STAIR WORKOUT X 3

For your first stair workout of the week, you'll take on a new challenge. First, warm up with the Rainier Dozen and some moderately-paced stair climbing. Then, your challenge is to do one burst of effort moderately hard, followed by a rest; then a second burst of effort very hard, followed by another rest; and then a third burst of effort where you make a close-to-maximal effort. In other words, you'll go from the bottom to the top of the stairs as quickly as you're able, or at least as fast as if you were being chased by a bear. This will end up looking like the following:

1. 2 minutes at 50-65% intensity, followed by 3 minutes of recovery (1 minute standing, 2 minutes descending)

2. 2 minutes at 65-80% intensity, followed by 3 minutes of recovery

3. 2 minutes at 80-90% intensity, followed by 3 minutes of recovery

For this week, repeat this cycle 2 more times for a total of 3. If 3 times is too many too soon, fall back to a consistent pace while stair climbing, or stop at 2 sets and work your way up next week. This is a very demanding workout, designed to mimic the physical stress that might be encountered on the mountain. Don't be discouraged if it takes a couple of weeks to work up to it. Remember to cool down with some walking.

An additional note on safety: after charging up the stairs at 90% intensity, your legs might be a little wobbly; so be extra careful not to trip while coming down the stairs.

Most people will experience some discomfort at this intensity. Remember that all of these workouts are challenge-by-choice. Whenever training for mountaineering, I always try to bear in mind that I'm responsible for my own safety and sometimes the safety of others. So even in training, I'm careful to not exert myself to the extent that I'll overextend or injure my body.

DAYS 3 AND 5: RAINIER DOZEN OR REST

Begin your day with the Rainier Dozen. Feel free to take another 30 to 60 minutes of light exercise if you feel like it (a brisk walk is a great option). It would also be good to take a complete rest day instead. Listen to your body. If you feel tired, rest.

DAY	WORKOUT	TIME & DIFFICULTY
1	Rainier Dozen + 30-Minute Easy Hike	42m Easy
2	Rainier Dozen + 1-2-3 Stair Workout x 3	1h17m Very Hard
3	Rainier Dozen or Rest	12m Recovery
4	Rainier Dozen + High-Intensity Stair Training x 7	57m Very Hard
5	Rainier Dozen or Rest	12m Recovery
6	Rainier Dozen + 1 Hour of Cross-Training	1h12m Medium
7	Rainier Dozen + 5-Hour Hike (9-10 miles, 35-pound pack, 2,500 feet elevation gain)	5h12m Hard
	TOTAL	9h44m

Table 11: Week 10 Workout Calendar

DAY 4: RAINIER DOZEN +
HIGH-INTENSITY STAIR TRAINING X 7

The high-intensity stair training that you were previously doing on day 2 moves to day 4 this week.

Warm up with the Rainier Dozen for 12 minutes. Then take 10 minutes to warm up on the stairs at a moderate pace. Perform each 30-45 second interval by running hard up the stairs at an effort level that feels like 85 to 90% of your maximal ability. Rest until your heart rate has come down to about 60% of maximum, about 3 minutes. Repeat the interval 6 more times for a total of 7 intervals in the workout. Cool down afterward with some walking or stretching.

DAY 6: RAINIER DOZEN + 1 HOUR OF CROSS-TRAINING

Warm up with the Rainier Dozen, and then spend an hour in some moderately vigorous cross-training activity. Listen to your body, and have fun with the workout.

DAY 7: RAINIER DOZEN + 5-HOUR HIKE (9-10 MILES, 35-POUND PACK, 2,500 FEET ELEVATION GAIN)

This week, after such a hard, new, stair workout, you'll keep the distance and difficulty of the hike the same. After warming up, hike for 9 to 10 miles, or about 5 hours. Try to use a location that allows you to gain about 2,500 feet of elevation. Keep the weight in your pack the same, 35 pounds, to account for the time you'll be on the trail, and pad your pack with additional gear or water if necessary to get closer to your target pack weight for this week.

SUMMARY

After the hike this week, some athletes may notice that they are really getting used to these workouts. As aerobic endurance increases and strength builds, you'll likely be finding that the workouts are more enjoyable and perhaps less taxing. On the other hand, you also added an intense new workout into your schedule this week, and some individuals may experience some fatigue. The important thing is to be in tune with your body. By this point, you'll also be getting highly organized with your equipment and clothing. Everything is falling into place.

WEEK 11

BRIEFING

The weekend hike will be 7 hours this week, and your day 2 stair workout will bump up to 4 sets of the 1-2-3 workout. Be sure to stay focused on your sleep and food intake this week, as you'll be burning a lot of energy.

DAY	WORKOUT	TIME & DIFFICULTY
1	Rainier Dozen + 30-Minute Easy Hike	42m Easy
2	Rainier Dozen + 1-2-3 Stair Workout x 4	1h32m Very Hard
3	Rainier Dozen or Rest	12m Recovery
4	Rainier Dozen + High-Intensity Stair Training x 8	1h01m Very Hard
5	Rainier Dozen or Rest	12m Recovery
6	Rainier Dozen + 1 Hour of Cross-Training	1h12m Medium
7	Rainier Dozen + 7-Hour Hike (12-14 miles, 40-pound pack, 3,500 feet elevation gain)	7h12m Hard
	TOTAL	**12h03m**

Table 12: Week 11 Workout Calendar

DESCRIPTIONS OF WORKOUTS

DAY 1: RAINIER DOZEN + 30-MINUTE EASY HIKE

Today's hike is a recovery workout, and you can also substitute it with a different activity, such as running, biking, or swimming. The important thing is to move at a moderate pace for 30 to 45 minutes.

The pace can be conversational, and you do not need to be dripping with sweat at the end of the workout.

DAY 2: RAINIER DOZEN + 1-2-3 STAIR WORKOUT X 4

Warm up with the Rainier Dozen and some moderately-paced stair climbing. Then, make 3 efforts: 1 moderately hard, 1 very hard, and 1 close to maximal effort, with rest periods in between. Repeat this workout 3 more times for a total of 4.

1. 2 minutes at 50-65% intensity, followed by 3 minutes of recovery (1 minute standing, 2 minutes descending)

2. 2 minutes at 65-80% intensity, followed by 3 minutes of recovery

3. 2 minutes at 80-90% intensity, followed by 3 minutes of recovery

DAYS 3 AND 5: RAINIER DOZEN OR REST

Begin your day with the Rainier Dozen. Feel free to take another 30 to 60 minutes of light exercise if you feel like it (a brisk walk is a great option). It would also be good to take a complete rest day instead. Listen to your body. If you feel tired, rest.

DAY 4: RAINIER DOZEN +
HIGH-INTENSITY STAIR TRAINING X 8

Warm up with the Rainier Dozen for 12 minutes. Then take 10 minutes to warm up on the stairs at a moderate pace. Perform each 30-45 second interval by running hard up the stairs at an effort level that feels like 85 to 90% of your maximal ability. Rest until your heart rate has come down to about 60% of maximum, about 3 minutes. Repeat the interval 7 more times for a total of 8 intervals in the workout. Cool down afterward with some walking or stretching.

DAY 6: RAINIER DOZEN + 1 HOUR OF CROSS-TRAINING

Warm up with the Rainier Dozen, and then spend an hour in some moderately vigorous cross-training activity. Listen to your body, and have fun with the workout.

DAY 7: RAINIER DOZEN + 7-HOUR HIKE (12-14 MILES, 40-POUND PACK, 3,500 FEET ELEVATION GAIN)

This hike, your longest yet, will require consideration of extra food and water, as well as considerations to ensure your clothes are comfortable and your feet are well taken care of. Consider taking an extra pair of socks to change into later in the day if your feet are tired or wet.

Warm up with the Rainier Dozen, and then hike for 7 hours, or about 12 - 14 miles, and for approximately 3,500 feet of elevation gain. Be sure to hike at an even pace. You should be carrying about 40 pounds by this point. So, if your 10 essentials, food, and clothing don't add up to that weight, consider adding some extra water for your ascent.

SUMMARY

It's normal to feel that you are pushing the limits. You are, and you'll do well to let friends and family know that this is an important time for you. Remember that during this phase you are intentionally going to the edge, which means that you are taking risks. Peak training requires meticulous attention to restoration and recovery. This is not a time to be burning the candle at both ends. Ample sleep, quality food, and good relaxation are your allies.

WEEK 12

BRIEFING

At this point in the 16-week training program, you are all in. This week adds a second hike to your weekend. For your long hike on day 7, you will be ramping up your pack weight to the most you will carry during the training program, an amount that likely matches what you will be carrying on your expedition. The day 2 stair session stays the same. You'll be adding a new kind of workout for a bit of variety: a fartlek hike on day 4, which will have similar training benefits to the high-intensity interval training you have been performing on stairs.

A fartlek is another version of an interval-training workout. The word originated in Sweden and means "speed play." It is popular with cyclists, runners, and cross-country skiers. You simply choose random targets like the top of a hill, a loop of a track, a tree, or trail marker and then get after it with gusto! Increase your effort level as high or moderate as you feel like, and mix up the length of the intervals. I like this type of training very much as it replicates the unpredictable nature of mountain terrain. It's fun, too, helping to pass the time while training alone or adding a competitive challenge with friends. If you don't have the time during the week to get out to a hiking trail, then use any uphill grade that is available. No matter what the terrain, you can always increase intensity by adding weight to your pack. Depending on the time of the year, terrain, and your preference, you may choose to wear a trail-runner shoe instead of a hiking boot for this workout.

DESCRIPTIONS OF WORKOUTS

DAY 1: RAINIER DOZEN + 30-MINUTE EASY HIKE

Today's hike is a recovery workout, and you can also substitute it with a different activity, such as running, biking, or swimming. The important thing is to move at a moderate pace for 30 to 45 minutes. The pace can be conversational, and you do not need to be dripping with sweat at the end of the workout.

DAY	WORKOUT	TIME & DIFFICULTY
1	Rainier Dozen + 30-Minute Easy Hike	42m Easy
2	Rainier Dozen + 1-2-3 Stair Workout x 4	1h32m Very Hard
3	Rainier Dozen or Rest	12m Recovery
4	Rainier Dozen + 1-Hour-30-Minute Fartlek Training Hike	1h42m Very Hard
5	Rainier Dozen or Rest	12m Recovery
6	Rainier Dozen + 3-Hour Hike (5-6 miles, 30-pound pack)	3h12m Medium
7	Rainier Dozen + 7-Hour Hike (12-14 miles, 45-pound pack, 3,500 feet elevation gain)	7h12m Hard
	TOTAL	14h44m

Table 13: Week 12 Workout Calendar

DAY 2: RAINIER DOZEN + 1-2-3 STAIR WORKOUT X 4

Warm up with the Rainier Dozen and some moderately-paced stair climbing. Then, make 3 efforts: 1 moderately hard, 1 very hard, and 1 close to maximal effort, with rest periods in between. Repeat this workout 3 more times for a total of 4.

1. 2 minutes at 50-65% intensity, followed by 3 minutes of recovery (1 minute standing, 2 minutes descending)

2. 2 minutes at 65-80% intensity, followed by 3 minutes of recovery

3. 2 minutes at 80-90% intensity, followed by 3 minutes of recovery

DAYS 3 AND 5: RAINIER DOZEN OR REST

Begin your day with the Rainier Dozen. Feel free to take another 30 to 60 minutes of light exercise if you feel like it (a brisk walk is a great option). It would also be good to take a complete rest day instead. Listen to your body. If you feel tired, rest.

DAY 4: RAINIER DOZEN +
1-HOUR-30-MINUTE FARTLEK TRAINING HIKE

Day 4 of this week is the first time you will try a fartlek workout. Warm up with the Rainier Dozen, and then hike for 1.5 hours. Depending on how you are feeling, occasionally pick a spot on the trail that feels an appropriate distance away, and sprint to it. Alternate these high-speed sections with walking at your regular hiking pace. You can choose the durations of the walking and sprinting sections as you like. At a minimum, you should allow your heart rate to recover to a conversational pace before taking on the next fast section. If you are doing the workout with friends, you can take turns picking the target.

DAY 6: RAINIER DOZEN +
3-HOUR HIKE (5-6 MILES, 30-POUND PACK)

The reason for back-to-back hikes this weekend is to mimic the actual Mount Rainier climb. You may be tired when you start the second and longer hike on day 7 or even have some muscle fatigue. The conditioning benefit from this is to get used to doing these long practice sessions so close together. By this point, you'll be getting so used to hiking that this won't seem like a significant challenge.

Warm up with the Rainier Dozen and then hike for 3 hours or about 5 to 6 miles. You may choose to include some pack weight up to 30 pounds if you like.

DAY 7: RAINIER DOZEN + 7-HOUR HIKE (12-14 MILES,
45-POUND PACK, 3,500 FEET ELEVATION GAIN)

This week, you will keep the length of your long hike the same, but increase the weight of your pack a little to simulate the pack you will likely carry on your summit climb. Warm up with the Rainier Dozen, and then hike for 7 hours, or about 12 to 14 miles, and try to gain 3,500 feet in elevation. Be sure to hike at an even pace, and include 45 pounds of safety gear, water, food, and clothing in your pack.

SUMMARY

Depending on where you have completed your workouts this week, you may have put boots on the trail 3 times in a week! Additionally, you will have completed a hike with a pack that weighs as much as the one you will carry up Mount Rainier. You are getting close to the levels of fitness needed for a successful ascent, as well as honing some skills of organization, mental toughness, and self-care that will pay off in the long run.

WEEK 13

BRIEFING

The hike you will do this week will be your longest one of the entire training program. You will complete an all-day hike and this will build both physical and mental endurance. The purpose of this hike is to replicate the summit climb of your expedition, which is coming up in 4 short weeks.

If you're local to the Mount Rainier region, you would be well served to visit Camp Muir for this part of the training. Make sure to follow the appropriate safety and permit-related guidelines when heading up there. If you're somewhere that doesn't have access to a long hike, this would be a good weekend to make a short road trip to a place that does. Either way, this will be a fun and substantial training session. The rest of your training this week will have modest increases over the previous week or will remain the same.

DESCRIPTIONS OF WORKOUTS

DAY 1: RAINIER DOZEN + 30-MINUTE EASY HIKE

Today's hike is a recovery workout, and you can also substitute it with a different activity, such as running, biking, or swimming. The important thing is to move at a moderate pace for 30 to 45 minutes. The pace can be conversational, and you do not need to be dripping with sweat at the end of the workout.

DAY	WORKOUT	TIME & DIFFICULTY
1	Rainier Dozen + 30-Minute Easy Hike	42m Easy
2	Rainier Dozen + 1-2-3 Stair Workout x 5	1h47m Very Hard
3	Rainier Dozen or Rest	12m Recovery
4	Rainier Dozen + 1-Hour-45-Minute Fartlek Training Hike	1h57m Very Hard
5	Rainier Dozen or Rest	12m Recovery
6	Rainier Dozen + 3-Hour Hike (5-6 miles, 30-pound pack)	3h12m Medium
7	Rainier Dozen + 9-Hour Hike (15-18 miles, 45-pound pack, 4,000 feet elevation gain)	9h12m Hard
	TOTAL	17h14m

Table 14: Week 13 Workout Calendar

DAY 2: RAINIER DOZEN + 1-2-3 STAIR WORKOUT X 5

Warm up with the Rainier Dozen and some moderately-paced stair climbing. Then, make 3 efforts: 1 moderately hard, 1 very hard, and 1 close to maximal effort, with rest periods in between. Repeat this workout 4 more times for a total of 5.

1. 2 minutes at 50-65% intensity, followed by 3 minutes of recovery (1 minute standing, 2 minutes descending)

2. 2 minutes at 65-80% intensity, followed by 3 minutes of recovery

3. 2 minutes at 80-90% intensity, followed by 3 minutes of recovery

DAYS 3 AND 5: RAINIER DOZEN OR REST

Begin your day with the Rainier Dozen. Feel free to take another 30 to 60 minutes of light exercise if you feel like it (a brisk walk is a great option). It would also be good to take a complete rest day instead. Listen to your body. If you feel tired, rest.

DAY 4: RAINIER DOZEN +
1-HOUR-45-MINUTE FARTLEK TRAINING HIKE

Warm up with the Rainier Dozen, and then spend up to 1 hour and 45 minutes on a fartlek training hike. Alternate sections of sprinting towards a target you select with walking at your regular hiking pace.

DAY 6: RAINIER DOZEN +
3-HOUR HIKE (5-6 MILES, 30-POUND PACK)

Warm up with the Rainier Dozen and then hike for 3 hours at a consistent pace. You may choose to include some pack weight up to 30 pounds, if you like, even though you may not need all of this weight for a mid-distance hike.

DAY 7: RAINIER DOZEN + 9-HOUR HIKE (15-18 MILES,
45-POUND PACK, 4,000 FEET ELEVATION GAIN)

Load up your pack to 45 pounds. Since you are getting pretty close to your actual climb of Mount Rainier, you'll want to get comfortable with the gear you'll be using, if you haven't already. At this point in the training, I like to add realistic weight: clothing, extra water bottles, perhaps even some summit gear like down parkas, heavy gloves, long underwear, and a helmet.

This is your longest hike of the entire training program, and you will do well to plan this hike as if you were planning your climb of Mount Rainier. Get all your gear ready the evening before and get a good night's sleep. Account for the time it will take you to get to the parking lot. Make sure to hike with a partner and let someone else know where you will be and what time you will be expected back. Take appropriate amounts of food and water to sustain you on the hike. Check the weather and take the right clothes with you. For more details on preparation for your hike, you may wish to re-read the chapters on "Self-Care and Recovery," "Nutrition: Fuel for the Journey," and "Equipment."

Warm up with the Rainier Dozen, and then hike for 9 hours, or about 15 to 18 miles. Try to choose mountainous terrain that involves an elevation gain of 4,000 feet during the ascent. Be sure to hike at an even pace.

SUMMARY

It's not uncommon for climbers to experience a very difficult day on this week's hike. At this point in the training, you are coping with fatigue. So, if you have a hard time on the trail, don't feel discouraged by your performance. You'll have a chance at another challenging hike next week, and you'll have the benefit of this week's experience.

If you do successfully complete this week's hike, congratulations! You're doing very well in your training and have completed one of the hardest weeks of the entire program. You are very well prepared for what lies in wait on Mount Rainier.

WEEK 14

BRIEFING

Do this week well and it may in fact be harder than the climb. This is the point; in an ideal situation, you want to make the training more difficult than the climb. Self-care, organization, and a positive attitude will play a critical role in the success of this week's training. Good luck!

Some clients have told me that the only easy day of this week was "yesterday"! During the first part of the week, you'll do the interval training you have become used to over the last few weeks, with the 1-2-3 stair workout. On day 4, you have a choice between high-intensity stair training or a fartlek training hike.

Heading into the weekend, over 3 days, you'll complete up to 13 hours on the trail. After this effort, the next big push you'll do will be on the summit climb. With the appropriate planning, you could turn days 5 through 7 into a 3-day backpacking trip. If you are able to, it wouldn't be a bad idea to take a day off from work so that you can focus on these tough back-to-back workouts.

Note that the hikes at the end of this week are steeper (in terms of elevation gain per mile) than previous weeks. Therefore, you may want to plan ahead to find particular locations that meet this criterion, as these steeper hikes will prepare you well for your summit.

DESCRIPTIONS OF WORKOUTS

DAY 1: RAINIER DOZEN + 30-MINUTE EASY HIKE

Today's hike is a recovery workout, and you can also substitute it with a different activity, such as running, biking, or swimming. The important thing is to move at a moderate pace for 30 to 45 minutes. The pace can be conversational, and you do not need to be dripping with sweat at the end of the workout.

DAY 2: RAINIER DOZEN + 1-2-3 STAIR WORKOUT X 5

Warm up with the Rainier Dozen and some moderately-paced stair climbing. Then, make 3 efforts: 1 moderately hard, 1 very hard, and 1 close to maximal effort, with rest periods in between. Repeat this workout 4 more times for a total of 5.

1. 2 minutes at 50-65% intensity, followed by 3 minutes of recovery (1 minute standing, 2 minutes descending)

2. 2 minutes at 65-80% intensity, followed by 3 minutes of recovery

3. 2 minutes at 80-90% intensity, followed by 3 minutes of recovery

DAY	WORKOUT	TIME & DIFFICULTY
1	Rainier Dozen + 30-Minute Easy Hike	42m Easy
2	Rainier Dozen + 1-2-3 Stair Workout x 5	1h47m Very Hard
3	Rainier Dozen or Rest	12m Recovery
4	Rainier Dozen + 2-Hour Fartlek Training Hike or High-Intensity Stair Training x 8-10	2h12m or 1h09m Very Hard
5	Rainier Dozen + 2-Hour Hike (3-4 miles, 1,500 feet elevation gain)	2h12m Medium
6	Rainier Dozen + 4-Hour Hike (7-8 miles, 45-pound pack, 2,500 feet elevation gain)	4h12m Medium
7	Rainier Dozen + 7-Hour Hike (12-14 miles, 45-pound pack, 4,500 feet elevation gain)	7h12m Hard
TOTAL		**18h29m or 17h26m**

Table 15: Week 14 Workout Calendar

DAY 3: RAINIER DOZEN OR REST

Begin your day with the Rainier Dozen. Feel free to take another 30 to 60 minutes of light exercise if you feel like it (a brisk walk is a great option). It would also be good to take a complete rest day instead. Listen to your body. If you feel tired, rest.

DAY 4: RAINIER DOZEN + 2-HOUR FARTLEK TRAINING HIKE OR HIGH-INTENSITY STAIR TRAINING X 8-10

This week, you have a choice between a 2-hour fartlek training hike, or 8 to 10 high-intensity stair intervals. Either way, warm up with the Rainier Dozen first before starting the high-intensity portion of the workout, and remember to cool down afterward with some walking or stretching.

DAY 5: RAINIER DOZEN + 2-HOUR HIKE (3-4 MILES, 1,500 FEET ELEVATION GAIN)

After a warm-up, hike for 2 hours, covering 1,500 feet of elevation gain. If you are absolutely not able to take some time off from work or otherwise fit in 3 consecutive days of hiking, you might opt to skip this hike and do 2 long days instead; that is, change the hike on day 6 to a 6-hour hike.

DAY 6: RAINIER DOZEN + 4-HOUR HIKE (7-8 MILES, 45-POUND PACK, 2,500 FEET ELEVATION GAIN)

This is the second day of your 3 consecutive days of hiking this week. Find a hike that allows for 2,500 feet of elevation gain and takes about 4 hours. Warm up with the Rainier Dozen, and then hike at a consistent pace. Carry a pack with you, with up to 45 pounds of weight, even though you might not need all of that food and water for the medium length hike.

DAY 7: RAINIER DOZEN + 7-HOUR HIKE (12-14 MILES, 45-POUND PACK, 4,500 FEET ELEVATION GAIN)

This hike is shorter in distance than last week but comes on the heels of 2 consecutive days of hiking. Pick a location that will allow you to cover 4,500 feet in elevation gain.

This will be your toughest hike or workout of any kind from here on out until your summit, so it's a great opportunity to practice packing well, exercising the right safety-related steps, and taking in the right nutrition. On the hike, keep moving at a consistent pace. Try out any gear that you've recently purchased to make sure it works well for you. Pay close attention to how you feel during the hike.

SUMMARY

Hearty congratulations! You've not only completed the toughest week of training but have completed the entire Peak phase. As you think forward to the next couple of weeks, one thing you should know is that you now fall firmly into the category of climbers who have what it takes to reach the top of the mountain on their first attempt. Previously, I discussed that statistically, slightly less than 50% percent of climbers are successful climbing Mount Rainier. So, you can see that you've come a long way.

Next week's training will be significantly different in that you'll be resting and recovering instead of loading up your body. It's also true that from this point forward, you really can't build any more fitness. The best part of this news is that you don't need to. You are ready.

CHAPTER 12
EXPEDITION PHASE

Pulse Check

As I discussed in the summary of the last week, you really can't build any more fitness between now and the climb. The other side of that coin is that there is the potential to squander the benefits you've worked for by doing too much. You'll note that there are no high-intensity workouts this week. Indeed, for some people, the hardest part of the week is managing the reduced amount of effort and intensity. In a very similar way to being stuck on a mountain waiting for a storm to pass, this week may test your patience, but you have to recognize that to overdo it now would be akin to stepping out into the storm. There is just no point.

The training intensity and volume are reduced roughly by 50%. Some ways to manage the additional downtime are by reviewing gear, reading about the climb, watching a movie, or catching up with friends and family. The last few weeks have been busy, and your climb is coming up at the end of the next week. It's time to relax.

SECTION 4 | THE TRAINING PROGRAM

As you look ahead at your schedule for the next 10 days, bear in mind that it's perfectly fine to juggle around days to suit your needs. It's certainly okay to skip training days if you need to. The goal from now onwards is rest and preparation. Depending on whether you are on a 4- or 5-day climb, you may be climbing at the very end of week 16 or one day into the week after. If you have an extra day off due to being local to the Seattle area and not having to travel, then feel free to perform some light exercise such as a short hike, or just take the opportunity to rest.

All the training has been leading up to Week 16. Most people are going to be a little nervous. If you're freaking out, now is a good time to actively practice relaxation and anxiety management skills. My frank observation is that no matter what concerns or doubts come up between the start and the end of this week, the right thing to do in almost every case is to relax and focus on the next hour. You will need all of your energy to climb this mountain. You should feel confident that the training you have will afford you the opportunity to reach the summit of Mount Rainier.

If at the end of this phase you stand on the summit of Mount Rainier, it will be because you put one foot in front of the other, over and over again, and met the challenge of climbing 9,000 feet from the alpine meadows of Paradise to the glacier-capped summit of the mountain. Along the way, you will find harmony with your teammates. You will boost them when they are tired, and they will do the same for you.

WEEK 15

BRIEFING

You'll scale back all of your training sessions in terms of volume and switch back to the easier stair training at a consistent pace. You'll still do a hike this week, but it will be only 4 hours, which, after the last week, should feel like a walk in the proverbial park! You'll take an extra day of rest from physical exertion on day 6, but you'll spend that time in the valuable activities of checking all your gear and making a list of all the food you'll need for the climb at the end of the next week.

DAY	WORKOUT	TIME & DIFFICULTY
1	Rainier Dozen + 30-Minute Easy Hike	42m Easy
2	Rainier Dozen + 1 Hour of Stair Interval Training	1h12m Medium
3	Rainier Dozen or Rest	12m Recovery
4	Rainier Dozen + 1 Hour of Stair Interval Training	1h12m Medium
5	Rainier Dozen or Rest	12m Recovery
6	Rainier Dozen + Equipment and Food Preparation Day	12m
7	Rainier Dozen + 4-Hour Hike (7-8 miles, 35-pound pack)	4h12m Medium
	TOTAL	**7h54m**

Table 16: Week 15 Workout Calendar

DESCRIPTIONS OF WORKOUTS

DAY 1: RAINIER DOZEN + 30-MINUTE EASY HIKE

Today's hike is a recovery workout, and you can also substitute it with a different activity, such as running, biking, or swimming. The important thing is to move at a moderate pace for 30 to 45 minutes. The pace can be conversational, and you do not need to be dripping with sweat at the end of the workout.

DAYS 2 AND 4: RAINIER DOZEN +
1 HOUR OF STAIR INTERVAL TRAINING

Warm up for about 10 minutes, and then climb up and down a set of stairs, at a consistent pace, for about 45 minutes to an hour. Cool down with some stretching.

DAYS 3 AND 5: RAINIER DOZEN OR REST

Begin your day with the Rainier Dozen. Feel free to take another 30 to 60 minutes of light exercise if you feel like it (a brisk walk is a great option). It would also be good to take a complete rest day instead. Listen to your body. If you feel tired, rest.

DAY 6: EQUIPMENT AND FOOD PREPARATION DAY

If you've already got all your gear ready, just use this as a rest day. Otherwise, using the lists provided by your guiding service, make sure to go through all your gear and verify that you have everything that you need. Check that your equipment is clean and in proper functional condition. Practice packing all this gear into your backpack to make sure everything fits correctly.

DAY 7: RAINIER DOZEN +
4-HOUR HIKE (7-8 MILES, 35-POUND PACK)

This is your last substantive hike before heading up the mountain. All you're aiming to do with this hike is to maintain the level of fitness you've worked so hard for over the last 15 weeks. As always, after warming up, hike at an even pace for 7 to 8 miles, or 4 hours. This is also a last good opportunity to test any gear that you might have recently acquired, so carry a 35-pound pack and make sure everything works well.

SUMMARY

By this time a week from now, you'll be at Camp Muir, just one day shy of your summit climb. For now, get plenty of rest, pay attention to nutrition, and know that you are ready.

WEEK 16

BRIEFING

There is no way you can improve your fitness this week. The purpose of each of the workouts this week is simply to allow your body to move, to feel the benefit of some light exercise, and to manage stress. Frankly, if any day this week you feel as if you would rather not exercise at all, you should make that choice.

DAY	WORKOUT	TIME & DIFFICULTY
1	Rainier Dozen + 30-Minute Easy Hike	42m Easy
2	Rainier Dozen + 30 Minutes of Stair Interval Training	42m Medium
3	Rest or Travel Day	Recovery
4	Orientation at Mount Rainier National Park	-
5	Full day of mountaineering training to prepare for the climb	-
6	6-Hour Climb to Camp Muir	6h Hard
7	Spend day at Camp Muir adjusting to altitude + Optional 2-Hour Hike	2h Medium
Next week + 1 day	14-Hour Summit Climb	14h Very Hard
	TOTAL	23h24m

Table 17: Week 16 Workout Calendar

Descriptions of Workouts

DAY 1: RAINIER DOZEN + 30-MINUTE EASY HIKE

Today's hike is a recovery workout, and you can also substitute it with a different activity, such as running, biking, or swimming. The important thing is to move at a moderate pace for 30 to 45 minutes. The pace can be conversational, and you do not need to be dripping with sweat at the end of the workout. If you don't feel working out, take a day off.

DAY 2: RAINIER DOZEN +
30 MINUTES OF STAIR INTERVAL TRAINING

You've cut the volume of this workout by 50%. You should also cut the intensity by the same amount. You've been training for close to 16 weeks and will be working hard on the mountain. You do not want to feel your legs burning in this workout, and you certainly don't want to deplete your energy stores. Have fun, celebrate your last stair workout, and maybe head to a nice restaurant with friends and savor the opportunity to eat with a knife and fork off a real plate.

Warm up for about 10 minutes and then climb up and down a set of stairs at a consistent pace for about 20 to 25 minutes. Cool down with some stretching.

DAY 3: REST OR TRAVEL DAY

Today may be a long travel day for you. If you're traveling by air, be sure to plan ahead to maintain your nutrition intake, paying attention especially to hydration. If you don't have to travel, consider today a bonus rest day.

DAY 4: ORIENTATION AT MOUNT RAINIER NATIONAL PARK

Today is a fun, technical-orientation day. You won't be required to make any exertions; simply take part in some enjoyable and informative sessions with guides to ensure that you have all the gear that you need and to practice getting it organized for the next few days.

DAY 5: FULL DAY OF MOUNTAINEERING TRAINING TO PREPARE FOR THE CLIMB

Today is a full day. Be sure to get up early, have breakfast, and pack sufficient food and drink in your pack for a full day on the snow. There won't be any significant elevation involved, and the purpose of the training is to build skills with the ice axe, crampons, and ropes. Even though there is no climbing per se, you will find yourself continually practicing with the tools and techniques taught by the guides. You'll be on and off the snow all day. As soon as you get back after this training, attend to any wet clothes that need to be dried and try to waste no time getting dinner and getting to bed. You have a big day tomorrow.

DAY 6: 6-HOUR CLIMB TO CAMP MUIR

You'll want to get up early again and have breakfast. Try to leave a half hour to relax before you head out to the mountain, which is around 8 am. You'll have an hour-long bus ride and all you'll have with you is your gear for the climb. You can take with you a bottle of sports drink or water to sip for the ride. From now until you get back down off the mountain, there can be no waking hours where you are not either eating, drinking, or getting ready to do both. This constant fueling is absolutely critical to success. There is a saying about this that goes, "In mountaineering, lunch begins when breakfast ends and ends when dinner begins."

Your main job today is to climb 4,500 feet in 5 miles. Your close second priority is to consume 4,000 to 5,000 calories, and to drink between 10 and 12 liters of fluids. No matter how much you like to eat and drink, this can be a pretty hard job.

On arriving at Camp Muir, sometime between 3 and 5 pm, your priority for the first hour should include drinking a liter of fluids, eating snacks, and practicing the pressure breathing that your guides will have been encouraging all the way up the snowfields. These activities are very important in warding off the effects of acute mountain sickness (AMS). The last two items on your agenda for today are dinner and a briefing by the guides of what to expect tomorrow.

DAY 7: SPEND DAY AT CAMP MUIR ADJUSTING TO ALTITUDE + OPTIONAL 2-HOUR HIKE

If you are on the 5-day climb, day 7 of this week comprises of rest, some easy hiking and possibly a glacier excursion, which is a nice way of stretching your legs and getting some fresh air in the lungs. However, the main purpose of this day is to rest, recover, and adjust to the altitude. If you are on the 4-day climb, this is your summit day, which I will describe in the next chapter.

SECTION 5

THE CLIMB

CHAPTER 13

SUMMIT DAY

Climb if you will, but remember that courage and strength are nought without prudence, and that a momentary negligence may destroy the happiness of a lifetime. Do nothing in haste; look well to each step; and from the beginning think what may be the end.

—Edward Whymper, *Scrambles Amongst the Alps*

REFLECTING ON THE PAST

For many years the above quote has been hanging in a faded plastic frame, nailed to the inside of the door of the climber's bunkhouse at Camp Muir.

It's a sobering reminder of what you are getting into. More people have walked out of Camp Muir than have come back. It's a big adventure, and it's happening now. No matter how busy I may be before setting off, I like to consider the women and men who've gone before, not just on this mountain, but since the first alpinists were heading out of the valleys of the French and Swiss Alps—heading skywards to peaks that had never been touched by hands or boots.

Everything we do today, every piece of equipment, and all of our collective experience have come from the pioneers who looked at those high jagged peaks with curiosity and wonderment, asking if they could be climbed. They were prepared to take risks and make a committed effort in order to follow the call of the mountains. This is not different than the effort you will make as you set off towards the summit of Mount Rainier.

Edward Whymper—the author of the quote at the start of this chapter—was an early pioneer of alpinism and earned the distinction of leading the very first team to the summit of the Matterhorn on 14 July 1865.

After three days of climbing along with 6 team-mates—Lord Francis Douglas, Charles Hudson, Douglas Hadow, Michel Croz, and two Zermatt guides, Peter Taugwalder (father and son of the same name)—Edward Whymper and his team left their camp at dawn, climbing from the Swiss side of the peak and reached the summit at 1.40 p.m. They celebrated and rested on the summit before beginning their descent. Shortly afterwards, tragedy struck. Hadow slipped and fell on Croz, who was in front of him. Croz was caught unawares and unable to withstand the shock; they both fell, and pulled down Hudson and Douglas.

Whymper wrote this account in a letter to the London Times:

For two or three seconds, we saw our unfortunate companions sliding downwards on their backs, and spreading out their hands endeavoring to save themselves; they then disappeared one by one and fell from precipice to precipice on to the Matterhorn glacier below, a distance of nearly 4,000 feet in height. From the moment the rope broke it was impossible to help them.

Often, 5 minutes before leaving, in the black of the night, I'll walk into the bunkhouse—suited up and ready to go—and read Whymper's words. I'll also ponder the fact that only 5 years after the first ascent of the Matterhorn, Hazard Stevens and P. B. Van Trump received a hero's welcome in the streets of Olympia after their successful Mount Rainier summit climb in 1870.

Mountain climbing is inherently dangerous. To discount this danger is foolish, yet to overthink it is to unnecessarily burn up important energy. On a spectrum between fearless and frozen, a good sweet spot is bold and humble. It's helpful to have enough tension to be alert, with enough confidence to be relaxed. Try to visualize this state and practice it in training. Imagine yourself stepping off onto the glacier with a sky full of stars and the dark valleys below. Your headlamp creates a pool of light ahead of you, with the sounds of gear clicking, crampons crunching in the ice, the weight of the mountain axe in your hand, and the gentle swoosh of the rope being pulled along the surface of the snow. You are trained and organized. You are walking into the night and ready for the day to come. Be deliberate, be relaxed, be in a state of flow.

FOCUSING ON THE DAY AHEAD

Waking up around midnight, it's easy to let the lizard brain take over and rush to get ready. First things first; as Whymper wrote, "Do nothing in haste."

Everyone has their own way of preparing and getting grounded. Take a few moments to get calm: a prayer, a meditation, a mental gratitude list, or the thought of a loved one always seems to slow a fast-beating heart and bring a smile to my face. Relax. Conserve your energy. Feel the magnitude of what you are doing and the beauty of your surroundings. Take a minute to get in the rhythm of breathing: deep, regular, and slow.

Did you sleep? Many people don't, and thousands of people have summited Mount Rainier with no sleep. You stayed up all night in college; you can do it on Rainier, too!

Your gear is mostly packed, so what's left is to get dressed, drink, eat, go to the restroom, put on your harness, spikes, and helmet, and then find your rope team. It's 45 minutes of work, and you have about 90 minutes in which to do it. Relax. If you have a problem or are worried about something, tell your guide. She or he is there to assist.

Remind yourself that you've trained hard for this, and your job is to be the best team member you can be right now. Your guides have a solid strategy, and they know what they are doing. What's important is to focus on the now. Make sure your clothes and boots are on comfortably. Check and double-check your crampons. Make sure you have your food, water, and sunglasses. At 10,000 feet, the air is thin, so keep focusing on deep regular breathing. Shoulder your pack, make your way to your rope, and clip in. Your guide will do a final check of harness and crampons and make sure you are securely attached to the rope.

There's a magical feel to Camp Muir before setting off. I often think of John Muir and his team getting ready to leave from here. It's fun to consider their climb all those years ago and the many people who have gone this way since. John Muir had just celebrated his 50th birthday a few months before the climb. Their climb took about 8 hours to the summit and another 6 hours down. Here is Muir's account of the camp now named after him:

> *Here we lay as best we could, waiting for another day, without fire of course, as we were now many miles beyond the timberline and without much to cover us. After eating a little hardtack, each of us leveled a spot to lie on among lava-blocks and cinders. The night was cold, and the wind coming down upon us in stormy surges drove gritty ashes and fragments of pumice about our ears while chilling to the bone. Very short and shallow was our sleep that night; but day dawned at last, early rising was easy, and there was nothing about breakfast to cause any delay. About four o'clock we were off, and climbing began in earnest.*

—John Muir, August 23 1888

THE CLIMB

So, the climb begins! In many sports, the last quarter is critical. In climbing, the first leg makes all the difference. The first leg can make or break the momentum needed for a successful climb. Keep a positive mental image of the climb as segments of 60- to 90-minute efforts followed by a short rest break. After 4 of these segments, you will reach the crater of the mountain. Weather, time, and energy permitting, another 30 to 45 minutes across the crater will take you to the true summit of the mountain, Columbia Crest at 14,411 feet. It is imperative that you focus on and climb the segment that you are in.

The descent generally takes about half as long as the climb. If you can stay focused on the segment-by-segment approach, you will find a way to overcome a multitude of challenges, some small and some possibly arduous, during the next few hours.

While no segment of the climb should be considered easy, the rest of this chapter is a rough breakdown of what to expect on the way to the top. As a disclaimer, note that the route changes daily, and your guide will prepare you for your chosen route. The glaciers change significantly from year to year as well, so the following is just a suggested guide of what to expect. I will describe the Disappointment Cleaver and Ingraham Glacier route since it is the one I've guided most often, and it is commonly used.

SEGMENT 1: CAMP MUIR TO INGRAHAM FLATS

- Time: 1 hour to 1 hour 30 minutes
- Start: Camp Muir, 10,060 feet
- Destination: Ingraham Flats, 11,000 feet

This leg starts out over the Cowlitz Glacier, which has a fairly shallow incline, before ascending the gravelly switchbacks of Cathedral Gap. Once at the top of Cathedral Gap, you'll have views of Little Tahoma and the upper mountain. From this point, you'll bear north and continue to ascend across rock and glacier to Ingraham Flats, where you'll take a break.

Going back to energy management, the key is to relax. Maybe you needed to go to the restroom at the last minute. Perhaps you have too few clothes, perhaps too many (use zippers to avoid sweating), perhaps your boot feels too tight or loose, perhaps you are experiencing general anxiety. In all of these cases, relax. Breathe. Calm your mind.

For me personally, I tap into the nature that surrounds me. Nature opens me up and allows my feelings and emotions to surface. There are very few hazards on segment 1; some potential for rock fall to the north, some crevasse obstacles underfoot, and some careful footwork required on the loose rocks of Cathedral Gap. Overall though, it's a chance to relax into the night and feel the joy of being high on a big mountain.

I had the chance to work on Mount Rainier after my dad Geoff died in 2003. I wanted space to honor our relationship and reflect on our friendship, so on each expedition that summer, I looked forward to the time spent walking across the Cowlitz Glacier between Camp Muir and Ingraham Flats. I had wanted to come to Mount Rainier with Geoff and for us to climb together—a plan that didn't materialize—so instead I'd try to imagine the way he would have seen it for the first time; the bright snow, the red rocks darkened by the night, the south face of Gibraltar Rock standing 2,000 feet above my left shoulder and blocking out the summit from view. With my axe in one hand and my fingers feeling the light tension on the rope behind, I'd think of ways to describe the starlight and storms to him, and in the solitude at the front of the rope, I'd let tears of joy roll down my cheeks. As I swung one leg beside the other, sauntering up and over the ridge of Cathedral Gap, I'd feel a sense of peace that made me feel loved.

Mountains are powerful. As you set out on this climb, use that power to lift your strength and spirit. At some point in the day, the mountain will likely lean on you. It will take a lot of strength to lean back. For this first segment, simply enjoy the magic of setting out. Try to find a rhythm. Find that state of peak-flow and let the mountain lift you higher.

Past the crest of Cathedral Gap, you will take a sharp left and head to the north. There's still some climbing left before reaching Ingraham

Flats, which is a large compression zone beneath the Ingraham Icefall. You'll pass Dunn's Corner, affectionately named after guide George Dunn who, while inspecting the route one night, got caught in an avalanche here and survived. At the time of writing George has reached the summit of Mount Rainier more than 500 times!

Enjoy the views ahead and the hundreds-of-feet-deep crevasses to the right. 10 or so more minutes and your guides will find a good rest spot. You've completed almost a quarter of the elevation of the day's climb.

SEGMENT 2: INGRAHAM FLATS TO TOP OF DISAPPOINTMENT CLEAVER

- Time: 1 hour 15 minutes to 2 hours
- Start: Ingraham Flats, 11,000 feet
- Destination: Top of Disappointment Cleaver, 12,300 feet

"Cleaver" is a Pacific Northwest term for a rocky ridge that splits a glacier into two parts. The mountain feature at the end of this segment isn't called Disappointment Cleaver because it's difficult. It actually got its name because when some early climbers were attempting the first ascent of this route, they reached the top of the 45-degree slopes and believing they were on the summit, began to celebrate. However, when the fog lifted, it exposed the 2,000 feet of ice above them. They called it a day and climbed down.

The break will have afforded you enough time to put on a parka, eat, drink, and adjust any gear. A glance towards the Ingraham Icefall and across to the Disappointment Cleaver indicates one thing: the warm-up is over. For many people, the next bit is the most arduous segment of the climb. It contains significant portions of glacier travel where one cannot stop or rest. This is followed by some challenging rocky terrain, which you will most likely navigate wearing crampons. It's tough to lead this segment, too; so, if you notice an uptick in the intensity of focus from your guide, it's because the next hour contains tricky terrain.

The first section towards the Ingraham Icefall involves a gently rising slope over the compression zone of the glacier. From there, the route traverses north and under millions of tons of broken ice. Your guide will prompt the team that during this section you must keep moving. The debris of ice and rock strewn around provides the explanation of why. This is not the most physically demanding traverse but one where a steady momentum is required to quickly pass through what rangers and guides refer to as the "Bowling Alley." Make each step count, move steadily, keep your wits about you, and stay alert for any instructions.

The trick to accomplishing this section well is to focus on breathing and relaxation. Try not to get flustered by the awkwardness of the transition from ice to rock. Most importantly, put your faith in your team leader. As you traverse all the way to the crest of Disappointment Cleaver, the hazards of the rock fall lessen. You'll make a sharp turn left and upward.

The guides know that this section is challenging, and they will do everything possible to provide coaching and encouragement to reach the top of Disappointment Cleaver without being overly fatigued. No one really wants to scramble over rocks using crampons and in the dark. Between the scraping noises, a spark from steel on ferrous rock, and trying not to bump into each other, this section can wear a person down. Again, relax; it's not a race.

The awkward rocks set people off balance, figuratively and literally. A marine explosives expert I was climbing with once said, "You know, I could bring this whole thing down to size and take out the rough sections." The environmental steward in me balked at that statement. The pragmatist in me said, "I like that idea!"

As you reach the break at 12,300 feet, take a deep breath and congratulate yourself. You are now just over halfway to the summit.

This is a critical recovery break. Not everyone will feel great. It may be difficult to escape the wind and cold. Your team leader may be looking for you to tell her or him whether you have what it takes to continue for several more hours to the summit. They are not trying to put pressure on you but simply making challenging assessments about how to manage resources most effectively. Staying here for more time than is necessary is not an option. It is usually too cold.

For many people who decide not to continue to the summit at some point during their climb, this is the turning point. It is a harsh fact of mountaineering that you could have done everything possible to prepare and have trained meticulously for this day, yet somehow today is not going your way. If today is not your day, then it is probably not the last day you will have a chance to try. Do the right thing, don't feel defeated, and know that the mountain will still be here next time.

SEGMENT 3: TOP OF DISAPPOINTMENT CLEAVER TO HIGH BREAK

- Time: 1 hour to 1 hour 30 minutes
- Start: Top of Disappointment Cleaver, 12,300 feet
- Destination: High Break, a range from 13,000 to 13,500 feet.

The challenging part of this segment is that you are now on the upper part of the mountain, exposed to all that the weather can throw at you. As you go higher, the air is becoming colder, and it is getting harder to breathe. Depending on the timing of the climb, it may still be dark; therefore, you will not yet have had the warming benefit of the sun. The good news is that you are climbing entirely on snow now, so you can get into a good rhythm and continue this all the way to the top.

As you climb higher, many people experience physical and emotional feelings ranging from hope to doubt, confidence to fear, being too cold to being too hot. You've come a long way and still have hours to go. This is where all of your training matters most. You may not be able to change any of these circumstances. However, with each step and each minute that you dig deep and find your reserves of strength and endurance, you can know that you're steadily moving towards your goal. It's not easy; if it were, there'd be a thousand other people up here. If there is one memorable thing about this section, it is the likelihood of seeing one of the most spectacular sunrises imaginable. Along with the sunrise, you may experience a small, but noticeable, increase in warmth. Many a climber has watched the horizon, a ribbon of crimson, pink, then orange. Soon the sun will show itself and take the edge off the bitter cold of the night.

The route on this segment changes weekly or daily. Seracs (pinnacles or ridges of ice) tumble, snow bridges give way, crevasses open, and everything morphs continuously all the way from spring to autumn.

Ladders, fixed lines, and route information passed between guides make it possible for rope teams to thread their way around seracs the size of apartment buildings and around crevasses big and deep enough to swallow a freight train. It's my experience that fatigue becomes a constant companion on this leg. You've been going for 4 or more hours, and from time to time it really is an uphill battle.

The rest point on this leg is called High Break. The dirty secret is that there is no specific feature on the mountain with this name. It's just a narrow shelf dug with shovels at an arbitrarily chosen spot around 13,200 feet. Needless to say, it's not much of a picnic spot. If you drop your pack or water-bottle, you'll likely never see it again.

It's normal to feel very tired here. The hypoxic environment (deprived of oxygen) degrades cognitive functions too, so rely on habits—put on clothes, eat, drink, breathe, focus on your needs, and steel yourself for the final push. Getting a wrapper off a candy bar with big gloves can seem extraordinarily difficult (use your teeth). Do whatever it is that you need to recompose yourself. I find that a quick meditation can help me get centered and focused here.

SEGMENT 4: HIGH BREAK TO SUMMIT CRATER

- Time: Approximately 1 hour
- Start: High Break, a range from 13,000 to 13,500 feet.
- Destination: Summit Crater, 14,100 feet

There is nothing easy about this segment. With fewer than 1,000 feet to reach the crater rim, and from having climbed all night, most of your team is experiencing fatigue. With the convex shape of the volcano whose top you are almost touching, it is very difficult to see just how far you have to go.

At sea level, I'm a big fan of enjoying exercise. I don't think you need to enjoy every minute of this hour for it to be a significant memory. In fact, some people might not enjoy it very much at all, yet you can feel proud of where you have climbed to. If you doubt your accomplishment, look for passenger jets flying south from the Seattle-Tacoma Airport, and notice that some of them are below your altitude. Think about that; you are two and a half vertical miles above sea level, and you climbed up here under your own steam!

A technique that will help to get through this segment is to break the section into manageable parts. This could be the distance to the next marker wand; it could be to simply put one foot in front of the other for another 5 minutes before counting out another 5. What's important to remember is that however slow your progress, very few people start this segment and do not go all the way. You have what it takes, and you are getting very close to the summit.

With 20 or 30 minutes remaining before reaching the summit crater, many people have told me that what kept them moving was to ask themselves how proud their loved ones would be if they could see them now. You will undoubtedly be tired and burning through fuel at a significant rate. It's hard to tough-it-out here and each step requires a solid effort. As fatigued as you may be in this segment, take time to remember the fundamentals: the rest step (a hiking technique your guide will have explained to you), pressure breathing, good posture, and energy management. Keep your head up. Smile. You're almost there.

Segment 5: Summit Crater to Columbia Crest and Back

- Time: Ranging from 5 minutes to 1 hour
- Start: Summit Crater, 14,100 feet
- Destination: Columbia Crest, 14,411 feet, or remain at Summit Crater

Few people have ever seen the inside of the summit crater of Mount Rainier. It's an awe-inspiring geological formation—approximately three-quarters of a mile across, filled with glacial ice and surrounded by a rocky crest that sits slightly higher than the crater floor. This route arrives in the crater directly opposite Columbia Crest, which is the true summit of the mountain at 14,411 feet. From the perspective of the National Park and the guide services, and for purposes of record keeping, to reach the crater is to reach the summit of the mountain. Get to here and your accomplishment will be noted in the National Park records forever.

You have two choices here, to rest and call this the summit, or to take the next 45 minutes to walk across the crater and ascend the short ridge to Columbia Crest. The way to make this decision is to consider how much is left in the tank. For many people, it's best to call this the summit, to rest, and to conserve energy for the climb down. In some cases, the mountain will make that decision for the entire team, because the weather will be so inclement that it is unsafe to venture further. If conditions are good, and you have reserves in store, drop your pack, put on a down jacket, and pick up your ice axe for the celebratory hike to Columbia Crest.

There is a rock called Register Rock on the opposite side of the crater. Beside this rock is a metal box chained to the ground containing a visitor book. 200 meters further is the highest point of the mountain, with a 360-degree view of Washington state, the Cascades, Puget Sound, and to the north, Canada. Congratulations, you have met your goal!

Segment 6: Summit Crater to Disappointment Cleaver

- Time: 1 hour to 1 hour 30 minutes
- Start: Summit Crater, 14,100 feet
- Destination: Disappointment Cleaver, 12,300 feet

For now, your well-deserved celebration can be held in store for your arrival back at Base Camp or when you reach town. The task ahead of you is to focus on the descent. After a quick safety briefing and a refresher on skills, you will head down the mountain. The descent happens quickly, and your training will pay off here, particularly your endurance, leg strength, balance, and coordination skills. Don't fight your momentum as you descend, and try to enjoy the flow of the rope team. The views are spectacular and the air is getting less thin with every step you take. Not long after the first hour has passed, you'll be sitting on top of Disappointment Cleaver again, and probably taking off layers as the air begins to warm.

Segment 7: Disappointment Cleaver to Ingraham Flats

- Time: 1 hour to 1 hour 30 minutes
- Start: Disappointment Cleaver, 12,300 feet
- Destination: Ingraham Flats, 11,000 feet

This is a tricky segment; you will want to pay close attention to footwork as your team maintains a steady momentum all the way to the break. Nearly everyone will be feeling tired now. Though you are almost at the end of your adventure, it's important to eat and drink at the last break; not necessarily because you feel like it, but to prepare your body for the next few hours to come.

SEGMENT 8: INGRAHAM FLATS TO CAMP MUIR

- Time: 45 minutes
- Start: Ingraham Flats, 11,000 feet
- Destination: Camp Muir, 10,000 feet

There are some potential hazards during this segment, and so you will want to maintain your awareness as you descend over Cathedral Gap and across the Cowlitz Glacier. However, the most treacherous terrain of the mountain is now behind you. As you near the end of this segment, you can start to relax and know that you are almost home.

SEGMENT 9: CAMP MUIR TO PARADISE

- Time: 2 to 4 hours
- Start: Camp Muir, 10,000 feet
- Destination: Paradise, 5,600 feet

After a break at Camp Muir to reorganize gear and pack for the final segment, you will soon head off as a team, down the mountain, on the final leg of your adventure. The break at Camp Muir is a transition. The climbing gear can be taken off and packed. There is no need for your helmet, harness, ice axe, crampons, ropes, and carabiners anymore. You'll be replacing insulating layers with lighter clothes, swapping your helmet for a sunhat, and replenishing the electrolytes, energy, and fluids that were expended on the slopes above.

This step represents a transition in terrain, as well. Above you is the austere, alpine, desert landscape where nothing lives or grows. Below are the alpine meadows, the sound of waterfalls, birds, bears, and marmots. John Muir so eloquently described this in *An Ascent of Mount Rainier*:

> *A garden filled knee-deep with fresh, lovely flowers of every hue, the most luxuriant and the most extravagantly beautiful of all the alpine gardens I ever beheld in all my mountain-top wanderings.*

The meadows of Paradise are aptly named. After a cold night on the mountain, with aches and fatigue, sore spots, skin tightened and burned by the wind, and feet ready to be free of boots, the meadows are rejuvenating and healing. In writing these words, I can almost smell the scent of beargrass, lupines, and firs. The hike from Camp Muir to Paradise takes approximately 3 hours for most parties, and there is a lot to enjoy along the way.

As close as it is, steel yourself for whatever conditions you'll encounter. Perhaps you will have a hot day and the air will be still. On a day like this, the guides can look to the horizon, pick the midpoint between Mount St. Helens and Mount Adams, and make a beeline for Paradise. On other days, visibility might make it impossible to distinguish between the ground and the sky, the wind may be blowing, and a wrong turn would be disastrous. The Muir Snowfield is a relatively straightforward climb or descent, but it is flanked by the Nisqually Glacier to the west and the Paradise Glacier to the east. Navigational mishaps in both directions have led to numerous tragedies. So, while the end of your adventure is near, and the biggest challenge is behind you, it's important to stay alert and be ready for whatever the mountain still wants to conjure up in terms of weather.

Be ready for a variety of underfoot conditions, too. I've heard that the Inuit people have over 100 words for different types of ice and snow. I'm not sure if "mashed potatoes" is one of those terms, but the Muir Snowfield at 2 p.m. on a hot day can make you feel like you are walking on mashed potatoes. This may not sound so bad to some, but the surface might be covered in hard, crusty ice. On some steps, you'll crunch straight through to firm ground below; other times it will give way awkwardly and you'll stumble. Sometimes you might end up flat-out on the snow after stepping on a hidden icy spot. It's the last stretch and your long day is almost at an end, but be sure to dig deep into your physical and mental reserves for whatever these last 5 miles deliver. It may well be that you'll end up using all of the skills that helped you on the upper mountain just to keep putting one foot in front of the other. Remember that what lies ahead are food, refreshments, a hot shower, and a soft bed.

SUMMARY

At the parking area and visitor center, turn around and look up at where you just came from and what you just accomplished. As kids eat ice-cream, tourists show genuine amazement for climbers coming off the peak. It looks so high and far away that it seems impossible.

If your energy stores are depleted, make sure to take the time to get some food and water in your body. Take care of any aches and pains, and try to get in a few stretches. As was the case in training and on the mountain, practicing self-care after your descent will set you on the road to recovery.

After every climb, I have a moment where I find it hard to fathom that just hours before, our team was standing on top of the mountain. I once had the chance to climb to the summit with a professor of literature. Upon arriving at Paradise, I asked him the question, "What is the correct literary description that applies to this experience?" He did not hesitate in replying, "Surreal."

The Merriam-Webster dictionary defines surreal as "marked by the intense irrational reality of a dream; unbelievable, fantastic." I can think of few other situations in my life experience where a single word has been able to so accurately describe an experience.

Something I've heard from many climbers is that this was the hardest thing they've ever done. It is truly a remarkable accomplishment to climb a mountain, and this is a jewel of a mountain. Nowhere in the world is there such a high peak so close to an ocean. No mountain in the lower 48 states is anywhere near as glaciated. I've had the chance to climb in many ranges, often on peaks higher than Mount Rainier. Yet, in three decades of climbing around the world, I've had some of my hardest days—and some of my most beautiful moments—on this peak.

I think that Mount Rainier can take us to the very edge of our mental and physical capabilities. I listened to Lou Whittaker, who founded Rainier Mountaineering, Inc (RMI), say once, "You can respect the mountain, but just remember, it doesn't respect you." I've felt emboldened, frightened, humbled, filled with joy and happiness, excited, subdued, driven, beaten down, fierce, worried, confident, strong, and weak on that mountain—sometimes all in the same climb. Mount Rainier has made me a stronger human and also a more grateful one.

Phil Ershler of International Mountain Guides often says to climbers, "You'll never again look at it from afar—and not feel like you came off it a little different than before you went up." That has been true for me, and I hope that it's true for everyone who takes this journey.

Congratulate yourself. It doesn't matter whether you turned around at the top, or somewhere before that. You made a full effort and took on a major challenge. Feel good about that and ask yourself, "What better thing could I have done with this day?"

Well done.

CHAPTER 14
EPILOGUE

*After climbing a great hill, one only finds that there are many
more hills to climb.*

—Nelson Mandela

It has been a joy to write *Fit to Climb*. I hope that you've found it useful, and I welcome any questions or feedback that you have. Our contact information is at the start of the book.

As I write these last few pages, I'm sitting in Seattle in a coffee shop. It's a beautiful late-autumn morning, with the sun filtering through maple trees. It's early, and the world hasn't quite woken up yet. It's only 70 miles to the mountain from here, but it might as well be on a different planet. Today's weather on the summit is forecast at 10 degrees with a wind speed of 60 miles per hour. That's chilly!

On Mount Rainier, I've pulled on spikes, tied into a rope team, and sauntered off across the Cowlitz Glacier well over 100 times. I once thought it would get easier over time, but it hasn't. I have prayed that one day it would not grip me with fear; that has never happened, and I'm pretty sure it never will.

There's no easy route to the summit. None. It's not ever safe, and it's not for the faint of heart. We can navigate well, we can practice, and we can mitigate risk, but we can't control it. And that's part of the beauty— the mountain is different every time. We won't know exactly what will happen until we get there.

Before a climb, especially the half hour before setting off, I feel a healthy dose of fear. It's normal. It's not "lizard-brain" paralyzing fear; it's more deep-rooted. It's a calm and clear fear, and it lingers like a soft ache. Recalling it now makes me ponder. It makes me push back from the table and take a deep breath.

Why do I have this fear? Simple—because the mountain is danger- ous. The weather does what it wants, rock falls happen anytime, and ava- lanches charge down the slopes. Sometimes the glacier surface opens up like a trap door, and then you fall. Hopefully, you don't hit the icy walls too hard or go all the way to the bottom. But even if your team catches your fall, you are still hanging on a half-inch-thick piece of nylon, looking straight down into a deep blue abyss.

I've run the gauntlet of getting on and off Disappointment Cleaver more times that I can remember. They call it the "Bowling Alley." A fall- ing rock nearby can be manageable, but it's never just one. Often, they come by the dozen. At best, it's unnerving; at worse, it's a bombardment.

On one summit climb, I got hit by a piece of ice about the size of a grapefruit that missed my helmet but hit my backpack. Not only did it smash my chicken sandwich and break my water bottle, it actually tore the strap away from the backpack before it slammed me onto the ledge I was perched on. It felt like a refrigerator had fallen on me. It knocked my breath away with an intensity that seemed to have a texture and color all of its own. I didn't see or hear it coming. A split second or 10 inches closer and... Well, the truth is, sometimes we are just lucky. I got back on my feet and kept on walking up the mountain.

We can't plan for these surprises, but we can prepare. We can do our best to mountain-proof ourselves, and that is why I wrote this book. I want you to stack the odds in your favor. I want you to train like you are preparing for the hardest thing you ever done. At the end of a climb, it's a comparison I've often heard.

I don't want you to train because you like it. As much as I enjoy the outdoors, I know that half of the time I'd rather do something less energetic. I want you to train to be able to move expeditiously through the hazard zones. I want you to train to have the balance and strength to be able to climb across a heart-attack-inducing, narrow ridge and not get blown off in the wind. I want you to train so that if you do have a fall, you can get the axe in the snow on the first, second, third, or however-many-it-takes time. Sometimes it's tough to get it to stick. That is a fight you have to win.

Train your body, train your mind, train your skills of packing, prepare, know your gear... and then keep training some more. Be ready for any card the mountain deals you, whether it be a sunny calm morning or a storm that sounds like a jet engine.

Adopt the mindset of a mountaineer from now on. Be that person who puts on his or her boots and pack and climbs up and down the office stairs at lunchtime. Be the person whose kitchen table is covered in maps and gear and Ziploc bags all packed a week before the climb. Be the mountaineer, who as Gaston Rébuffat quoted, "is the person who drove their body where once only the eyes could see"—and returns.

Feel the passion. Feel the fear. Feel the pull of nature, and feel your strength. Let it all propel you forward in your training and preparation. If it gets overwhelming, take a deep breath and focus on the thing you are going to do in the next 5 minutes. If you doubt your ability, try doubting your limits instead. Most of all, feel the drive and hunger for adventure that was in you before your bones began to grow.

If you are reading this book, you've likely already made the decision to try and climb the mountain. Don't worry about the summit, focus on giving all of your attention to the process. As one climber told me,

"Sacrifice yourself on the anvil of effort." Don't worry too much about the plan; it will change, and you will adapt. You will. Before you are halfway through, you'll be a stronger, quicker athlete, and you will have more endurance than you can imagine now.

When you get to the mountain, put your boots on the snow, turn your eyes upward, find strength in your legs, and joy in your heart. Take a deep breath and set the dream free. Let that beautiful mountain lift you up into the night sky.

To the top!

37 THINGS THEY NEVER TELL YOU BEFORE YOU CLIMB

The following are some words of wisdom that your guides have learned from many trips up and down the mountain but may forget to tell you! Not all of them may apply to your situation, and it is certainly possible to overcome some mishaps. However, given the challenging experience you are about to undertake, you should do everything you can to maximize your comfort, the performance of your gear, and your fuel. These tips are organized into 3 sections: self-care, equipment, and nutrition. I hope you find them helpful.

SELF-CARE

1. Some amount of fear and anxiety is normal. You are going into the unknown. Remember that thousands of people have done this before. Trust your guides.

2. While on the subject of trusting your guides, communicate with them about how you are doing at all times.

3. If you are susceptible to blisters, pre-tape your feet with athletic tape. Learn and practice how to do this during hikes.

4. See your dentist. On the mountain, issues with teeth are often exacerbated by the cold and the altitude, so attend to dental issues well before the climb to minimize unnecessary discomfort!

5. The drug Acetazolamide (sold under the brand name Diamox), which is commonly used for altitude sickness, is a diuretic, which means that it promotes the production of urine. Climbers using it will need to intake additional water and salts in order to compensate.

6. Some women have reported menstruating earlier than expected on the mountain. Guides will often carry extra feminine hygiene products, but if you prefer not to ask or want your own brand and type, prepare to carry your own just in case.

7. A white baseball hat with a dark brim underneath will reflect the sun away from your face.

8. Hold onto your hat if a helicopter is landing nearby.

9. Put sunblock on and in your ears, on your nose, underneath your nose, and slightly up your nose. Apply constantly and keep the sunblock handy. I recommend Dermatone because it does not come off with sweat.

10. Use a wax-based lip cream with sunblock that does not come off with sweat (Dermatone makes this product, too), and keep it near at hand as well.

11. If you wear contacts, be careful while putting sunblock on your forehead. Sunblock will fog your contacts and can irritate your eyes. Consider using a headband or a hat.

12. If you wear contacts, carry extras in a hard case. A soft case will get crushed. Keep them as well as a small bottle of contact liquid handy. Dry air and dust, which are plentiful on the mountain, cause havoc with contacts. More than one climber has failed to summit because things went awry with their eyes and contacts.

13. You cannot get warm standing still on a mountain. You can only retain heat from your previous effort. When you stop higher on the mountain, put on your warm clothes.

14. Don't leave your warm clothes in Paradise because it was 90 degrees Fahrenheit there! It is not warm higher up the mountain.

15. You do not lose a third of your heat through your head—this is a myth. Do not rely on your head gear alone to keep you warm overall.

16. Make sure your undershirt or upper base layer is long enough to tuck way into your pants. The action of your harness and your backpack will cause it to ride up, exposing your bare skin to the elements.

17. Don't avoid going to the bathroom. If you hold in urine, it will cool your body down, causing a loss of energy. It is also uncomfortable. If you need to pass a bowel movement but hold it in, this will lead to constipation and dehydration. Figure out what works in training.

18. It is acceptable to have a 1 liter pee bottle for use in the vestibule of the tent. A wide-mouthed bottle is a good choice.

19. Never look down into the toilet; you could lose your headlamp.

20. Wash your hands with soap and water after using the toilet even if the water is cold. A little soap and rubbing with snow will work.

21. The corollary to this is: don't share food with someone who hasn't washed their hands. Transmission of bacteria through food is a common way that climbers get sick on the mountain. To be safe, if you are sharing food, pour some of it out into the other person's hand or utensil instead of letting them reach into your food bag.

22. The temperature and the dry air will cause the skin on your hands to crack. Slather your hands with a thick hand cream and stick them right into the gloves. You cannot protect your hands too much.

EQUIPMENT

23. If you wear insoles during training, be sure to wear them on the mountain.

24. There is no such thing as a waterproof backpack. You must line your pack. Everything in your pack should be in a liner or in a Ziploc bag. The best liner is a trash compactor bag. It's a 0.3 mm bag, and it won't tear; you can buy 5 for less than $10 at your local big-box grocery store.

25. Snow will get into your backpack when you open up your pack, especially in a driving snowstorm. Protect your gear. Melting snow will wet anything that is unprotected.

26. Your ski parka will not work for mountain climbing. Do not make substitutions with equipment your guide service recommends. There is a very good reason it is on the list, and you are a long way from a store such as REI. Don't endanger yourself and your chance at summiting, or risk severe discomfort, by using the wrong equipment.

27. Consider using clear goggles at night to protect against dust.

28. Waterproof gloves do exist. They are called Sealskinz (http://www.sealskinz.com/US/). If you suffer from Raynaud's syndrome, consider using these gloves.

29. Consider lightweight gardening gloves for hot conditions. They are tough, and will protect your hands from the rope, ice axe, and rocks.

30. Consider a good pair of outdoor-activity-specific underwear that is soft and wicking. Seams and poor choice of materials will chafe, adding to your discomfort. Try these out in training.

31. When you only need one of an item on the mountain, share everything you can with climbers in your group.

32. Duct tape is handy for quick fixes on the mountain - wrap a small roll around your hiking poles to keep it accessible.

NUTRITION

33. There are some things you probably don't want lining the inside of your pockets because of the potentials for messes. A short list includes torn carbohydrate gels, mashed bananas, melted chocolate, peanut butter, jelly, or a leftover sandwich. You are a long way from a washing machine! Besides the discomfort due to the smell, you want to get in the habit of keeping clothes free from food odors. Sooner or later you may be in bear country and you don't want to smell like a tasty bite. Fortunately, there are not many bears above the tree line in Mount Rainier National Park.

34. You cannot have too many Ziploc bags to organize your backpack. Organize your food into snack sized baggies: 1 break, 1 bag.

35. Freezer bags are sturdier than regular Ziploc bags, and are less likely to tear when you open them or to split under the weight of other items in your pack.

36. If you wake up in the middle of the night and are cold, eat something.

37. Watch out for the foxes! They will eat your food. There are a lot of animals on the mountain who would like to share your food, and you want to avoid this happening. One obvious reason is that you need the food. In addition, on an environmental-care note, you do not ever want to feed the wildlife; it results in horrible problems for the animals. Ravens, grey jays, marmots, and foxes are all highly adept at stealing your food. The birds will actually unzip your pockets if you leave a backpack laying around. Marmots are cute but not overly aggressive. I'm most impressed by Arctic foxes who will often intimidate an unsuspecting climber while they are eating. The best result possible (for the fox) is that you panic and drop your food. I saw a fox drag an entire food bag across a snow-slope once, a herculean feat for the animal and not a happy situation for its owner. During my tenure as a Rainier guide, we used a "fox box" (plastic lockable container) for food. It had marks on it that looked suspiciously like the teeth marks of a fox!

ABOUT THE AUTHORS

JOHN COLVER

John Colver has two decades of international experience leading high-altitude expeditions, including 8 teams and over 100 people to the top of Tanzania's Mount Kilimanjaro, the highest point in Africa, and 5 teams each to Alaska's Mount Denali and Argentina's Mount Aconcagua, the highest points in North and South America, respectively. He has guided with leading US guide services Rainier Mountaineering, Inc. and International Mountain Guides, on over 100 Mount Rainier summits.

John discovered a passion for mountaineering as a teenager, and never stopped climbing. He emphasizes exercising outdoors, drawing inspiration from nature to inspire action, and a commitment to a life of fitness. He is an award-winning athletic coach, former mountain guide, former competitive cyclist, award-winning author, and outdoor-adventure advocate. Since 2001, as a fitness coach, John has coached over 2,000 clients of all ages to various goals ranging from 5-kilometer to 100-mile races, cycling and triathlon events, climbing major peaks, and simply enjoying fitness activities. John currently lives in Portland, Oregon.

ROHIT EIPE

Rohit Eipe met John in 2009 and has trained with his fitness training programs ever since. He is an enthusiastic runner, having completed 3 marathons and several races of other distances. He enjoys running and hiking outdoors throughout the year and is planning to hike Mount Rainier in summer 2018. He works as a Software Engineering Manager at Amazon and lives in Seattle, Washington with his partner Maya Smith.

INDEX OF FIGURES

INDEX OF TABLES

Made in the USA
Las Vegas, NV
15 December 2021

37736861R00132